When The Holy Dances With The Ordinary

I0152057

Cycle A Sermons based on the Gospels for Advent, Christmas and Epiphany

Christopher Keating

CSS Publishing Company
Lima, Ohio

WHEN THE HOLY DANCES WITH THE ORDINARY

FIRST EDITION
Copyright © 2025 by
CSS Publishing Company, Inc.

Library of Congress Cataloging-in-Publication Data
Names: Keating, Christopher W. author
Title: When the holy dances with the ordinary : Cycle A sermons based on the gospels for Advent, Christmas and Epiphany / Christopher Keating.
Description: First edition. | Lima, Ohio : CSS Publishing Company, [2025]
Identifiers: LCCN 2025029387 (print) | LCCN 2025029388 (ebook) | ISBN 9780788031274 paperback | ISBN 9780788031281 adobe pdf
Subjects: LCSH: Advent sermons | Christmas sermons | Epiphany season--Sermons | Common lectionary (1992). Year A
Classification: LCC BV4254.5 .K43 2025 (print) | LCC BV4254.5 (ebook)
LC record available at https://lccn.loc.gov/2025029387
LC ebook record available at https://lccn.loc.gov/2025029388

For more information about CSS Publishing Company resources, visit our website at www.csspub.com, email us at csr@csspub.com, or call (800) 241-4056.

e-book:
ISBN-13: 978-0-7880-3128-1
ISBN-10: 0-7880-3128-7

ISBN-13: 978-0-7880-3127-4
ISBN-10: 0-7880-3127-9

To my wife, the Reverend Carol McCracken Keating,
with much love and gratitude for your patience, laughter,
faithfulness, and support. I could never have imagined a better
life and am thankful for the ways you have taught me to see
glimpses of the holy in the ordinary moments of life.

Contents

Introduction

Discovering The Holy In The Ordinary: Reading Matthew In Winter

"We have seasons when we flourish and seasons when the leaves fall from us, revealing our bare bones. Given time, they grow again." (Katherine May, *Wintering: The Power of Rest and Retreat in Difficult Times*)

Katherine May's spiritual reflections on winter are as intriguing as they highlighted often ambiguous lessons the colder season teaches us. She reminded us that there are seasons of our lives when the warmth of the sun falls fresh on our faces offering gifts of brightness and renewal. And then there's winter. Winter brings moments of stone-cold barrenness. Stripped of our reserves, we are plunged into a season of vulnerability, exposed to the raw elements. Those in cold weather climates know the drill. November's autumn glow changes quickly into a barren landscape. Assaulted by arctic blasts, our skin becomes pale and scaly, our joints stiff. Yet even the coldest winters will yield to spring, and even the barren trees still find ways to shout their praise. The grass withers, and the flowers fade, but hope abides. Given time, May said, and even these bare bones moments will be enfleshed once more.

Our hope in winter emerges from moments of ordinary grace: a kettle of soup shared with a neighbor; cups of coffee warming hands after worship; a roaring fire warming spirits after long days; a mission project followed by a church supper.

It's significant that the church year also begins in winter, offering reminders to us that possibilities often lie beneath barren soil. Joyce Rupp called this the "strengthening darkness," which reminds us we "are the terminal buds waiting in repose, to be energized in our vigilant dormancy."[1]

With that in mind, the church year begins by reading Advent's apocalyptic dreams that will gestate into new possibilities. The birth of Jesus brings amazement and terror, a reminder that God's possibilities always threaten the status quo. Soon enough, we follow Jesus as he is immersed into the waters of baptism and sent into the wilderness of temptation. Eventually, we journey with him up the mountain of Transfiguration where we once again await signs of God's power.

The lectionary is our guidebook through these festivals and ordinary moments. It offers a contrast to the culture's movements during the same period. The world moves quickly from fall to winter, shifting from pumpkin-spiced days to glittery and garish celebrations, concluding with over-hyped football championships and promises of Valentine's Day's chocolate-enhanced romances. Meanwhile, the church understands something about the possibilities of winter that the culture does not. The very things that our culture yearns for — community, wholeness, resilience — are found not in wrapping ourselves in fleece and comforters, but in the church's fellowship and proclamation. More is happening in winter than meets the eye. The holy is dancing in those regular days when a grilled cheese sandwich and a cup of tomato soup seem to be the only things that satisfy.

Like Mary, the church is called to ponder this wondrous message of light and hope dancing together during days when daylight seems scarce. Sometimes even hope itself seems scarce. Sometimes the grilled cheese sandwich sticks to the bottom of the skillet. In W. H. Auden's memorable words, "We have seen

1   Joyce Rupp, "A Winter Prayer: Strengthening Darkness," https://joycerupp.com/a-winter-prayer-strengthening-darkness/#:~:text=O%20Strengthening%20Darkness%2C%20we%20are%20the%20terminal%20buds%20on%20the,come%20again%20into%20our%20lives.

the actual vision and failed to do more than entertain it as an agreeable possibility, once again we have sent him away."[2]

During winter, the church is called to listen to a message that moves from angelic proclamations to thundering mountain top pronouncements and everything in between. After the brightly colored decorations are packed up and put away, we find ourselves pondering, treasuring, and wondering how hope remains. Often it appears in an ordinary way, the same way infants have always been born. The child lies in a rough manger, with hands out-stretched, inviting those who are watching to dance with joy.

Reviewing the gospel lessons for the first part of Year A has helped me discover new glimpses of the mysterious and holy lurking around the edges of the everyday ordinary. These are lessons infused with images of the holy inviting the ordinary to dance, or perhaps vice versa. The texts guide our winter pilgrimage from Advent through Epiphany. When we finally ascend to the summit of the Mount of Transfiguration, our eyes once more see the promise of God shining against the backdrop of our fragile world. No wonder Peter wants to capture that moment by starting a building campaign. His weary eyes want to behold that vision of the holy forever.

Matthew's gospel will prove to be a reliable companion for these winter months. Much like winter, Matthew's gospel seems to be straddling both the past and the future. Matthew's audience, scholars believe, consisted largely of Jewish converts to Christianity. They brought with them a religious heritage influenced by the Hebrew scriptures as well as Jewish spirituality and devotion. In this wintering moment of their lives, Matthew's church is faced with questions of what it means to reconcile what Tom Long called "the relationship between the old and the new, between the cherished traditions

2   W.H. Auden, "Christmas Oratorio," at https://allpoetry.com/Christmas-Oratorio

and commandments of their Jewish legacy and the new demands of Christian discipleship.[3]"

While we do not know much about Matthew's audience, it does seem as if they were caught by blizzards of change and upheaval. They were a community in transition, wrestling with new identities while struggling with the experience of being ostracized from other Jewish communities. That may feel a bit familiar to those of us in the twenty-first-century church. We stand in those liminal spaces, caught between the realities of a changing world and a beleaguered church. Not unlike our congregations, Matthew's church understands firsthand the difficulties of discipleship in a changing, pluralistic world. The gospel offers us glimpses of how it learns from its failures, while leaning into a vision of participating in the mission of God.

In other words, Matthew's church is learning how to embody the sacred mission of God within the context of their ordinary human lives. They are discovering the dance steps that creates and sustains the movement between the holy and the ordinary. Matthew offers the contemporary church instructions about that dance as it moves into the world. For Matthew, that dance begins with Jesus' family tree where the lives of ordinary men and women interact with the giants of Israel's story. These unlikely dance partners find themselves summoned by the Spirit to acts of generosity and heroic praise.

The dance continues as mysterious visitors travel by starlight to find the baby Jesus, before it changes into a mournful procession of grief as mothers cry out for their murdered children. When the holy and the ordinary dance, the church discovers the presence of Christ standing within both the anguish and beauty of human life.

Warren Carter noted that Matthew's gospel, which is the primary gospel for Year A, was a narrative focused on advo-

3   Thomas G. Long, *Matthew*, ed. Patrick D. Miller and David L. Bartlett, *Westminster Bible Companion* (Louisville, KY: Westminster John Knox Press, 1997), 2.

cacy and hope. It was an account of those summoned by God to stand fast on the promises of God by resisting the allure of the empires of the world. [4] Those promises, often expressed as the "kingdom of God," emerged from the margins of ordinary brokenness, disappointment, and struggle. That struggle then becomes a choreography of sacred hope which resists the pressures of Roman imperial power and the cultural structures of the synagogues that had ostracized Matthew's audience.

These lectionary passages have helped me, and my congregation, to be attuned to the gospel's blending of the holy and ordinary. This realization first dawned on me some years ago a few weeks before Christmas. 'Twas the second week of Advent, and the pastor was stirring. Panicking is a better word. With just days to go before the annual children's pageant, I was still struggling to recruit a full cast.

Finding Mary and a host of angels had never been a problem. The same was true for shepherds and kings. The real problem was locating Joseph. Few boys were comfortable with the idea of standing next to a girl who was said to be carrying their child. Whoever the scribe was who crafted the script for our annual pageant had managed to keep Joseph's lines to a minimum. But, at the very least, old Joe had to stand proximal to Mary, who was assumed to be great with child.

In my experience, most elementary-school-aged boys found that to be deal-breaker. Simply standing in front of the church for most of the worship service made them uneasy; standing next to a girl who was alleged to be carrying their child was too much. Still, I made a series of inquiries. I could hear one boy screaming "no, no, no," in the background. Another suddenly caught the flu. Others were out of town. A few never returned the call.

That left a young man whose mother had just started attending church. She eagerly "voluntold" her son for the job. She actually seemed excited — which is not the way I'd de-

---

4   Warren Carter, *Matthew and the Margins*, (Sheffield Academic Press, Sheffield, England, 2000), p. 1.

scribe her son's response. "I'm sure he'd be thrilled," she said, though I was much less confident. Nonetheless, I relaxed. "Hallelujah," I said. Immediately I posted "Habemas Joseph," a play on the Latin words spoken following the election of a pope, on the church's Facebook account.

When he showed up on Sunday, it was clear he would rather be anywhere but Bethlehem. He looked like a conscript in a guerilla war, or a mobster summoned to testify before Congress. It was painful to watch.

"He looks like he's being held hostage," our youth minister whispered to me.

I expected him to take the fifth instead of reading his line. The congregation giggled at the incongruity of Joseph frowning at the sight of the birth of our Lord.

But it is also possible that the original Joseph might have had a similar reaction. Faced with an unbelievable set of facts, I think Joseph would have had a hard time balancing the holiness of the moment with the practicalities of caring for a new family.

I can imagine Joseph balancing feelings of both fear and anger. That also strikes me as one of the ways we experience grace. His unvarnished fear of participating in something beyond his immediate control, something he neither sought or even desired reminded me of the ways we experience the incarnation. God appears in unlikely places, and then invites us to dance. These experiences are beyond our comprehension. No wonder Joseph was confused.

When I think of the way the holy dances with the ordinary, I think about that boy. (For the record, that was his first and last appearance at church.) I hope that in some way the mystery and confusion of the incarnation became real to him. Then I think about the original Joseph, the righteous, strong, silent spouse. I imagine him struggling with not exposing Mary to disgrace or feeling embarrassed by the village rumor mill.

Push the image a bit further and consider the other ways the ordinary and holy mix in Matthew's gospel. Astrologers traveling far and wide by the light of a mysterious star; an angry, narcistic despot triggered by the notion that an infant king could challenge his authority; frantic parents rushing to grab their belongings before fleeing their homeland. Wrap your head around those varied images while also looking for the places God shows up.

Jesus, walking along shorelines and through villages, teaching in synagogues and breaking bread with the poor. Watch as he brings healing to the brokenhearted and listen as he speaks words of mercy and forgiveness. Tax collectors leave their booths, and those who were fishing drop their nets. All through the gospel, Jesus shows up to announce the reign of God, calmly saying, "Follow me." In response to the holy, ordinary persons change their careers. The afflicted find healing, and a new community is formed. Time and time again, holiness appears in ordinary moments, and the dance continues.

Some years ago, a group of us were reading *Unbinding the Gospel,* Martha Gay Reece's study on evangelism in the mainline church. You read that right: it's a book about evangelism in mainline churches. Reece's thoroughly practical and hopeful research explores the possibilities of how mainline churches might engage in their own dances with that elusive, sometimes terrifying "e-word." She dispels the myth that mainline churches can't do evangelism effectively, while also challenging congregations to do more. She drives home the notion that upholding mainline identity and progressive values is not antithetical to practicing evangelism.

Toward the end of the book, she offered a chapter on the nuts and bolts of effective evangelism. She called it, "The Holy And The Practical," presenting it as a reminder that too often churches emphasize one at the expense of the other. When our group read that chapter, it was as if someone had flipped a switch. Patterns we had previously missed emerged as fresh possibilities. Our passion for teasing out the ways the sacred interacts with the practical reignited.

"A soul is linked to a body," said Reece. The sacred dances with the ordinary through the "practical structures of sermons and small groups, newcomers' dinner parties and signs for the parking lots. The holy is encased in the pragmatic."[5]

The trick is finding ways to allow the holy and the practical to dwell together. Reece noted that while some churches are disconnected from the power and mystery of the holy, losing sight of the mystery of faith, others become so consumed by the mystery they turn inward, losing focus. Instead of separating the two, Reece urged congregations to find ways to "hold the opposites together." She added, "It's all mystery. It's all practicality. All the time."[6]

The idea of holding that tension together has continued to be a hallmark of our ministry and were the spark behind the sermons in this collection. Keeping our eyes peeled for the ways God's holiness dwells with us in the ordinary moments of life leads to new ways of reading scripture. One of the astonishing expressions of the Incarnation is trusting the Spirit's invitation to dance, even for someone like me who has two left feet.

I remember watching my parents dance. They grew up in the swing era of big band ballrooms and continued enjoying dancing throughout their lives at weddings and banquets. That's the invitation I hear in these texts. These stories ripple with images of the holy dancing with the ordinary in our world. The Spirit takes the lead, enabling us to see God's grace appearing in new ways.

Forty-two years ago, I summoned my courage to ask another first-year student at Princeton Theological Seminary to a Halloween dance. She surprised me by saying yes, which was especially gratifying since I had broken our first date so I could go to a movie with some other guys from our dorm. Two years later, Carol McCracken Keating and I were married.

---

5   Martha Gay Reece, *Unbinding The Gospel*, (St. Louis, MO: Chalice Press, 2007), p. 105.

6   Reece, *Ibid.*, p. 106.

Throughout our marriage, Carol has embodied grace, taught me courage, and revealed the light of God to me and to our four children. I'm forever grateful to God and to Carol for all she has meant to me, and I lovingly dedicate this volume to her. My thanks to the members of Woodlawn Chapel Presbyterian Church in Wildwood, Missouri, where these sermons originated. Additional thanks to the ever-patient David Runk at CSS Publishing, and to treasured study group colleagues whose insights and ideas are a constant help in ironing my theological wrinkles. My deepest gratitude to Tom Willadsen for his careful reading and comments. As always, I remain indebted to countless teachers at the University of La Verne, Princeton Theological Seminary, and Saint Paul School of Theology.

All of these and many more friends and family have been wise and loving dance partners. Together we have beheld the glory of God, and the promises of Christ, even though I still have two left feet.

It's Time

"But about that day and hour no one knows, neither the angels of heaven, nor the Son, but only the Father...(v. 36)

Mariah Carey fans eagerly await the arrival of November 1 each year. For them, it's not just All Saint's Day, but a day nearly as important as Christmas itself. It's the day the queen of R and B releases a new video introducing her irrepressible Christmas anthem, "All I Want for Christmas." Fans hold their breath all year in anticipation of the singer's shrill exclamation, "It's *time!*"

It all began some years ago when Carey off-handedly uploaded a homemade cell-phone video to Instagram as a way of telling fans they could start playing her beloved song. The video went viral, of course, immediately spawning a new Christmas tradition. Every succeeding video has become more elaborate, all of it building to her majestic proclamation: "It's *time!*"

It's like horse racing's call to the post. It rings out across the Internet and is broadcast on airways everywhere. Radio stations shuffle their playlists to an all-Christmas format, and coffee shops introduce holiday cups. Our Halloween decorations are still hanging on the front door, but everywhere else it is Christmas time.

Yes, it's time...time for parties and presents, decorations and get togethers. It's time for a high-octane holiday explosion, glitter and glamour galore. It's time for light displays and inflatable Santas, prancing reindeer and caroling parties. It's time for cookies and candy canes, time for well-rehearsed family rituals, and even time for outsized expectations and painful struggles.

All that creates a problem, of course, because while Mariah Carey fans have begun celebrating Christmas on November 1, the church waits until Advent is completed. It's Christmas time...here, there, and everywhere — except, of course, at church. That is especially true for churches that maintain a stringent Advent observance. In some congregations, this extends to a near-total ban on the singing of Christmas carols prior to December 24. While the culture is awash with the songs of Christmas, these congregations remain steadfast in singing anything but Advent songs.

I don't intend on engaging in that debate — except to say that more people are familiar with Christmas music than they are with Advent hymns! But no matter what songs our congregations sing in December, Christians know that a new season begins the first Sunday of Advent.

It is indeed time — not for Christmas, but for Advent. The days of Advent differ from Christmas time. Advent, with its purplish hues, penitential longings, and spiritual expectations, contradicts the twinkling, consumer focus of Christmas. Advent time challenges us, said Walter Brueggemann with the reminder that "we may be visited by a spirit of one-ness, generosity" which "may cover over us, carry us to do obedient things we have not yet done."[7]

This colliding of two different ways of telling time is never easy to explain. I once attended a worship service celebrating a pastor's last Sunday with a congregation. Though he was much beloved by the congregation, he was apparently a purist when it came to not singing Christmas music during Advent. During the farewell, tributes to the pastor were offered and memories shared. But then one woman from the choir stood up and said, "We'll miss you, but at least now we can sing Christmas music in December!"

7 Walter Brueggemann, *Celebrating Abundance*, (Louisville, KY: Westminster/John Knox Press, 2017), p. 5.

The challenge is real. Pastor and author MaryAnn McKibben Dana, suggests that the temptation for church leaders always seems to be finding a way of not getting too carried away in the "kitschy detritus and overconsumption" of Christmas. Yet the flipside, she noted, can become a strict liturgical correctness that is missed on the wider culture. There is real danger, she said, in putting Christmas music on hold for weeks, only to crank it up on December 24, the very moment "when people may be sick of hearing them thanks to so many mall PA systems."[8]

A church I once served received multiple complaints from neighbors when its expensive carillon system broke in the middle of December. Neighbors flooded the church office with phone calls following eight hours of being deluged by "O Holy Night." The nonstop nocturnal caroling had left the neighbors with a disagreeable opinion of Presbyterians. Even worse, the music had become increasingly distorted as the night wore on and the device continued to fail. By dawn, they were hardly of the mind to give their church neighbors a favorable Yelp review. They weren't quite ready to hand us over as martyrs but were coming close. Some of Jesus' traumatic predictions were beginning to ring as clear as the church's chimes — a reminder that Christians are certainly called to pay attention.

Understanding what time it is during Advent goes deeper than monitoring what music is played. Jesus' instructions in Matthew call us to cultivate an Advent practice of paying close attention to what is happening around us. Knowing how to tell time during Advent includes holding in tension the great mystery of faith: Christ has died, Christ is risen, Christ will come again." And so we begin, not by singing loud carols or even watching an infant wiggle around a straw-filled manger. Instead, we bend our ears to hear Jesus' instructions on how to patiently endure the terrifying signs of the end of the world.

8   MaryAnn McKibben Dana, "We Need A Little Christmas, Right This Very Minute" https://nextchurch.net/we-need-a-little-christmas-right-this-very-minute-on-singing-christmas-carols-in-december/, accessed 9/18/2024.

Without batting an eye, Jesus looked at the disciples and told them "Pay attention, because it's going to be a wild ride." Jesus pulled no punches as he highlighted the ugliness and chaos that would threaten to overtake the faithful. Walking outside the temple, he pointed out the buildings elaborate ornaments and carvings. "Even these will soon be nothing more than a pile of rubble," he told the disciples.

Such talk is disturbing. Yet Jesus' apocalyptic imagination is grounded by the reminder that God remains firmly in charge of what is about to happen. Any of us might come unglued by Jesus' descriptions of what was about to happen: nations rising against nations, kingdoms battling kingdoms, not to mention famines and earthquakes. His words were and are terrifying, but the kicker is that "all this is but the beginning of the birth pangs."

None of this will happen on a predictable schedule, either. While Christians throughout the centuries have always yearned to pinpoint the exact date and time when the world will come to end, Jesus reminds us that is a fool's errand. Such talk will lead them astray, distracting them from the purpose he calls them pursue: to endure so that the good news may be faithfully proclaimed. Indeed, as Jesus has said, "the one who endures to the end will be saved."

Apocalyptic passages like Matthew 24 often results in Christians shaking their heads in disbelief while others are scurrying around frantically worried that they will be somehow left behind. Others of us wilt from seriously contemplating apocalyptic. But the word means "revealing," or "uncovering." Jesus' words are not meant to frighten or amuse (much like those old bumper stickers that said, "Warning! In Case of the Rapture, This Vehicle will be Unmanned!"). Instead, Jesus' words reveal the hope at the center of Advent.

Yet do not be misled, he reminds us. Many will try to lead you astray. Many will fill your heads with stories aimed at generating fear and anxiety. Many will hope that your lives will be distracted from the ways of faithful discipleship. Such preachers have always been lurking near the edge of the gospel, yet their contentious conspiracy theories and rumors offer no lasting hope. Only those who remain watchful and aware of what time it really is, says Jesus, will remain focused on the kingdom building tasks he has taught.

Jesus' words echo what we hear from the prophet Isaiah today. We hear Isaiah's baritone announce something even more important than Mariah Carey's kitschy catch phrase. He cries out with the reminder that God's people are called to pay close attention. "In days to come the mountain of the Lord's house shall be established," he cries out. The venerable King James Version adds even more poetic urgency: "And it shall come to pass in the last day."

Yes, yes, yes, it shall come to pass. Here is where Advent's apocalypticism grabs us by the collar and calls us to pay clear-eyed attention to what is happening. It's time.

It's time — time to be fully aware, yet also fully assured.

While he was dying of cancer, the late Catholic theologian Richard Gaillardetz wrote that "one of the gifts of a terminal cancer diagnosis is the entirely new relationship to time it affords us. Even under such a diagnosis, I still don't know my allotted time, but the relentless aggressiveness of pancreatic cancer does not encourage optimism regarding a long-deferred passing."[9] Yet this knowledge did not foster a sense of despair for Gaillardetz. Instead, he wrote, "Advent demands a wager. If I learn to cultivate this gratitude for the Christ abiding in the 'now' of my life, the lurking anxieties and fear of death this cancer mounts against my soul will lose their sting."[10]

It's time — time to live with an urgency of hope built on the assurance of God's lasting promises. Matthew's visions build on what scholars call Mark's "little apocalypse," (Mark 13). Here, Matthew provides pastoral assurance to a congregation riddled by anxiety and confused by Jesus' delay in returning.

9   Richard Gaillardetz, *While I Breathe I Hope*, (Collegeville, MN: Liturgical Press, 2024), p. 37.

10 *Ibid.*, p. 58.

The faithful remain alert and prepared, confident but not anxious, continuing to do the sorts of things disciples are called to do: showing mercy, offering kindness, acting with justice.

Matthew gathers these words of Jesus as a way of urging restraint and promoting hope among believers. Jesus, he reminds us, will indeed return. We are called to live with that assurance, and are thus advised to avoid either frantic worrying or passive neglect. Instead, Jesus tells us, the responsibility of disciples is to know that now is the time to pay attention.

Such is the nature of apocalyptic. It calls forth an Advent of waiting and earnest preparations. It speaks to the "hopes and fears of all the years," calling our attention away from that which is temporary to the lasting hope of the kingdom. Within the New Testament, apocalyptic stories and writings convey a unique sense of the end of time. While some hear these stories as literalistic narrations of God's pending judgment, Jesus calls us to take them as hopeful reminders of God's steadfast love. Emmanuel, God with us, is still here. Do not worry, but instead pay close attention.

It's *time*, Jesus tells us. And while it may not seem like the sort of Christmas message we might put on our a church Facebook page, the reality is that this is exactly the message our world yearns to hear. Like the neighbors besieged by a broken church carillon, our world is tired by the endless repeating of empty messages. Even the spectacle of viral videos wears thin. The centrifugal force of cultural Christmas pulls at us, causing us to neglect what is truly important and lasting.

Jesus' message to us this Advent is good news indeed. It echoes Isaiah's prophetic announcement. "Pay attention," Jesus tells us, "Because it's time to get to work."

He reminded the disciples to remain attuned to what was happening. He invited them to set aside notions of certainty in favor of focused discipleship. Likewise, Jesus reminds us to pay attention, to avoid becoming so mired down by the anxieties of life and worries of the world that we miss the signs of what is about to happen. It's time, he told us, though he quickly adds the less-than comforting caveat that "about that day and hour no one knows, neither the angels of heaven, nor the Son...keep awake therefore for you do not know what day your Lord is coming" (24:36, 42).

It's *time*, he said.

But if his assurance does not immediately sound like tidings of comfort and joy, then consider how this message is consistent with the entirety of Jesus' message. Jesus' words to the disciples were an invitation to ground their lives in the disciplines of readiness and anticipation. Here, on the precipice of his passion, Jesus reminded us once more that disciples are called to be salt of the earth, lights shining in the world, wise servants whose lives reflect God's intent for the world. He prepared the disciples to be people who know what time it as they eagerly await God's coming kingdom.

Unfortunately, the kingdom of God does not arrive with the promise of next day delivery. It's a struggle the early church learned, and a struggle that has continued for centuries. It is a struggle today.

Struggling with telling time is partially the result of the world's reliance on faulty clocks. The time-telling technologies of our world are never in sync with God's timing. We have seen it as our mission teams have encountered areas impacted by natural disasters, or as we have made attempts at unraveling the tightly bound webs of systemic racism. Those ensnared by the barbed wire prongs of evil are left wondering how long they will need to wait. Jesus told us that it was time, but still the question remains, "Time to do what?"

In his book *Spare*, Prince Harry recounts his memoir of life as the son of the current King of England. As a young man, Prince Harry struggled with his path in life, ultimately choosing to serve as a helicopter pilot in the Royal Army. Yet even a prince does not just show up on an airfield and become a pilot. The path involved rigorous training, beginning with a particularly tough flight instructor who gave Prince Harry his first flying lessons. After weeks learning the basics of take offs and landings, the grizzled RAF veteran turned to Prince Harry one day while they were flying and told him, simply, calmly, "Sir, it's time." Prince Harry's eyes narrowed. "Time for what?" he replied. "It's time for you to fly solo, to take controls." The instructor showed no hesitation or worry — and was more assured than the prince himself. The time had come for the instructor to step aside to allow the student to fly alone.[11]

This is the sort of focused urgency that Jesus foisted on us. Calmly, yet authoritatively, he told the disciples, "It's time." There's no guarantee of success, of course. But for that reason, the work of paying attention is so much more urgent. This is not a time for driven scampering around, but instead a moment of deliberate focus. He told them, "When you see all these things you know that it is near, right at the door" (Matthew 24:33, NIV).

It's time. Not just any time, but Advent time. Advent is a time for not rushing into endless choruses of "This Christmas," or whatever else gets blared across airwaves. It is instead a moment for telling time differently. It is a season for paying close attention.

Advent begins as the church lights a single candle. It flickers in the wind, its light barely sufficient against the overwhelming darkness. By this solitary reminder, however, we know that it is time to remember that light which is coming. It's time remember the possibilities of God dwelling with us. It is time to remember that great mystery of faith — Christ has come, Christ has died, and Christ will come again.

Amen.

---

11 Prince Harry, *The Duke of Sussex, Spare*, (New York: Random House, 2023), p. 162.

Second Sunday of Advent
Matthew 3:1-12

Tugging At Santa's Belt

"In those days John the Baptist appeared in the wilderness of Judea, proclaiming, 'Repent, for the kingdom of heaven has come near'..." (v. 1)

I was coming close to the end of that magical time of life when visits to see Santa Claus no longer held the allure they once did. I had graduated to the ripe old age of seven or eight, and while I was still wanting to hedge my bets, I had little desire to actually sit on the guy's lap. But neither did I want to shut down the notion of Santa Claus completely. I just wanted to meet him briefly, sort of a causal meet-and-greet, perhaps like a business networking opportunity. Maybe we could grab some eggnog and have a chat about the reindeer. Or even a quick handshake, a wink, and a nod.

But...my mother warned, "No photo!"

Wondering if I should let go of my childish ways, I stood in the line by myself as my mom wandered away to do some shopping. Who could imagine that happening today? Anyone leaving a child in a line full of strangers who were waiting to sit on the lap of a man whose last known address was "The North Pole" would be reported to the authorities. But then we also played with lead soldiers and sharp-pointed yard darts. I took my place in the line.

I doubt that the line was as long as the queue that formed around John the Baptist in the wilderness. Matthew told us that Jerusalem and all Judea was waiting in line, drawn by his quirky personality and rapier-sharp proclamation. I imagine parents were wrangling children, slicking back cowlicks, and straightening up cloaks in preparation for baptism.

Tall for my age, I surely stood out among the other kids. I was barely eight years old but was almost as tall as some eleven- or twelve-year-olds, making my presence in the Santa line seemed a bit unlikely. I harbored a strange mix of feelings. I wanted to be present, but also felt uncomfortable, even uncertain. I kept rehearsing my lines: "I want a Matchbox® racing set, and my mother told me to let you know we don't want any expensive pictures!"

By the time our children came along, the annual trek to see Santa had morphed into an all-day family event. Much to the despair of our older girls, my wife and I insisted on maintaining the tradition longer than they wished. Our youngest son still delighted in Santa, even though his sisters' interests had shifted. Unlike my mother, my wife *wanted* the picture, and so each year we waited in that long line so they could tug on Santa's belt.

Despite our daughters' protests that they were much too sophisticated to be seen gathered around Santa, we maintained the tradition. Their arguments finally stopped the year we encountered a family all dressed in matching candy cane striped pajamas — Mom, Dad, and each of the five kids. From toddlers to teens, all attired in green and red formfitting Spandex®. Our daughters froze, their mouths wide open. My wife turned to our girls and said, "Girls, your lives could be much, much worse."

These are the cherished traditions of December: waiting in line, tugging on Santa's belt, whispering in the old elf's ear as an assistant snaps a photo. Enthralled by the scenery and decorations, little ones cough up their Christmas confessions, hopefully loud enough for both Santa and parents to hear.

John's appearance in our annual Christmas pageants carries similar overtones. For Matthew, John the Baptist was a bit like a gate that swings open to the arrival of Jesus' message. He showed up as an appetizer before the messianic meal, whetting the people's spiritual appetites and fostering their awareness of God's kingdom. Likely, the crowds gathered there would have experienced many of the same feelings I experienced waiting for Santa — those strange feelings of anxiety, anticipation, queasiness, perhaps even dread. Slowly they make their way toward this odd character whose very dress and message invoke images of Israel's great prophets.

This time, however, there are no photos or posed portraits. Instead, one by one, the crowds make their way toward the river. Something remarkable happens, said Matthew. John's old school prophetic message was infused with the message that something new was about to happen. He announced that there was one coming who would be even more powerful than he. "He will baptize you with the Holy Spirit and fire," he declared.

This message is disturbing. Here was not a well-dressed elf surrounded by a professionally decorated set. John may have a beard and wear a belt, but that's where the comparisons to Santa end. His unkempt hair and scraggly beard would get him sent home by Macy's. Indeed, there is little about John that is cozy and welcoming. "Charming" is not a word that comes to mind as you look at his scratchy camel hair tunic and breath smelling of sweet insects. He shouts out at us with terrifying honesty. Are we prepared for the coming of God?

I'll tell you the truth: in all the years I've been associated with children's Christmas pageants, there is never anyone who signs up to be John the Baptist. We have a hard time getting anyone to play Joseph, likely because the script calls for Joseph and Mary to hold hands. John the Baptist is a whole other level of strange. You won't find Target selling nativity scenes featuring John the Baptist, and you certainly don't see Martha Stewart dipping bugs in honey for her Christmas tea. They don't make Hallmark Christmas movies about John, and we do our best to give him as little airtime as possible.

Here's the truth: John was indeed the odd cousin cast in the Christmas pageant. He truly was one crying in the wilderness, his voice is far removed from the places we usually visit at Christmas. The wilderness is far from the neighborhoods filled with twinkling lights, far from the citadels of power, and farther still from shopping malls and center of holiday commerce. His was a voice that did not seem to count, a voice without credentials.

But listen to what he was saying. Take a few minutes to strain your ears to hear John's distant wilderness howling. He proclaimed words of challenge, of change, but words we deeply need to hear. His words invade our ordinary celebrations and call us to pay attention. You would certainly pay attention if a family showed up to church today wearing candy cane striped stretch pajamas; so perhaps it is equally as important to listen for John's voice.

Matthew invited us to tug at John's belt, because that might make the biggest difference in our lives this Christmas.

There is something significant that John's message begins with a call to repent. Repentance is rarely found on our Christmas wish lists, but our lives are diminished if we fail to heed its poignant Advent invitation. These hectic, frantic days are filled with all sorts of preparations: wrapping, baking, buying, cleaning. But perhaps we ought to push the pause button on those activities, and circle back to the very basic, yet counter-cultural message of John. Let's begin with repenting—a true shifting of our minds and a changing of direction.

Those who were tugging at John's belt discovered the freedom provided by confession and repentance. John's voice called forth the coming of the kingdom of God. He instructed those who had come to the wilderness to begin preparing for that kingdom through acts of confession and repentance.

It's a message many have experienced within the sanctity of Alcoholics Anonymous. I have heard many AA members describe their participation in recovery in terms similar to religious conversion. "I once was lost, but now am found," many say. It's a reminder that repentance is not merely saying sorry but is instead a decision to embrace a new way of living. Turning from the pain of addiction, those in recovery discover the freedom and healing of grace.

It is a word of good news that echoes across the valleys of time, rising from the ancient rivers of Jordan into the highways of Advent. Today, John invites us to tug a bit on his belt and hear the message of God resonate within us: "Repent! The kingdom of God has come near!"

He knows that the presence of God is about to appear, and he calls all those who will listen to prepare. It is a remarkable sermon that is proclaimed from the heart of grace. It is a message that radiates from the promise of a God who journeys with those who are in pain. To repent is not to grovel our way back to God, sniveling and sniffling because we have made a mess of ourselves. To repent is to hear John's declaration of newness, and to seek his promise of redemption. To repent is to align ourselves with the possibility that God is present in the ordinary struggles we face daily.

Notice how Matthew contrasted John with another bombastic character in the gospel, King Herod. Herod's paranoia and fears dominated much of Matthew's early chapters. But while Herod could order troops into battle or send goon squads on murderous missions, John possessed a different sort of power. He lacked the royal robes and was not girded with swords and amulets. He could not issue decrees, nor could he march troops to the front lines. But even though John lacked imperial power, crowds still clamored to hear him preach.

They eagerly awaited his message. They came, confessed their sins, and received his baptism. Think about that for a moment: no preacher in America today could garner large crowds by wearing strange outfits and challenging the authority of the government. John was a strange character, yet his message drew crowds from across the area. Perhaps this is what prompted Jesus' question in Matthew 11:7 "What did you go out into the wilderness to look at?"

John was a wild beast of a man, a strange character who bore little resemblance to conventional preachers. His message was hardly a homiletical prize winner, either. It lacked any complex structure, and fell short on illustrations. There were no jokes, no cute stories about little kids, and no flowery quotations of poetry. His words were neither warm nor friendly; they were certainly not the sort of "seeker-sensitive" language contemporary preachers use to attract new members. His tone was sharp, his message direct: repent. Change directions. Come back to the God who has loved you. Come to the God who loves you still — but be willing to change everything about the way you live your lives. Confess your sins and live by the covenant of God.

John's words functioned as the appetizer for that main course that is still to come. In fact, Matthew reminded us that Jesus' own ministry began by borrowing a line from his cousin's sermon: "Repent, for the kingdom of God has come near."

Repent is hardly the sort of word we expect to hear in Advent. It carries overtones of guilt and harsh indictments. But the crowds who have gathered around John came there because they knew something was not right in their lives. Somewhere, perhaps deep inside of them, they knew something was missing. It was that longing that sent them to tug at John's belt.

They came from places of privilege and power, as well as pockets of poverty and weakness. They were the religious elites who had discovered that their wisdom no longer satisfied their longing hearts. They were thieves and tax collectors, over-powered narcissists and abusers. They were longing for light, for hope.

He told them: "Repent, if you are overconfident about your understanding of faith. Change your mind if you have no room for doubt. Repent, if you have allowed your privilege to hurt others. Repent, if you discover that loving your neighbor also includes standing near someone you despise. Repent over your lack of concern for the environment, or for your apathy over systemic injustices. Repent, and remember that forgiveness is the cornerstone of faith.

Let me offer a thought: while we wait to tug at Santa's belt, we are mainly preoccupied with finding new ways of saying, "Gimme...Gimme...Gimmee..." We may not deserve to be on the nice list, but our hunch is that sweet talking the old guy might just work. God, on the other hand, beckons us toward a new way of living. Here is a gift we truly do not deserve, given without consideration of who we are or what we have done. It comes to us as a gift without a price — except that we repent.

Of course, repentance is not easy. It requires that we ask for help. It is not a passive action but is instead an active turning toward God. It is a conscious decision to embrace the way of life that Jesus described as the kingdom of God. It means shedding our pretense and letting go of our notion that we can make it through life by ourselves.

It requires walking toward the voice crying in the wilderness, so that we may receive the gift he offers. It leads us to Bethlehem and, beyond — always calling us trust, to believe, to turn toward God and remember we are loved, even if we don't buy those expensive photographs.

Amen.

Find Your Joy

Strengthen the weak hands and make firm the feeble knees. Say to those who are of a fearful heart, "Be strong, do not fear! Here is your God... (Isaiah 35:3)

Not long after Carol and I started dating, I was giving her directions on how to navigate one of New Jersey's notoriously complicated highways. The basic rule of driving in New Jersey is to go as fast as you can, as far as you can, and remember that any time you need to turn left you have to first turn right. I believe it is codified in New Jersey's constitution. Anyway, I was giving her directions when she quickly stopped me. "Why do you, and for that matter all the other Californians we know in seminary, talk about highways that way?" I was puzzled. "What way?" "All the Californians I meet always put a "the" in front of the name of the highway as if it's their personal highway!"

If you've ever seen that old Saturday Night Live sketch, "The Californians," then you will know what she was talking about. Californians have a special attachment to their favorite freeways and nearly always add the article "the" in front of the freeway's name. So, for example, headed into Hollywood for Pasadena you take the 210 to the 134 to the 101 — if you're lucky. Or you could go the long way around on the 210 west to the 110 south to the 5 north. Californian's navigate freeways with the confidence of Isaiah 35:8, "no traveler, not even fools shall go astray."

Or so you'd think. Not long ago, I was visiting family in California. I found myself flying down those familiar freeways. There I was...driving down *THE* 805, and flying past *THE* 8 and suddenly, I missed my exit. How did I know that I missed my exit? Because the next sign I saw said "International Border ahead." My sister's house was close to Tijuana; you could, in fact, see the lights of the hills of Tijuana from her backyard. But I knew enough to know that I did not want to take the 805 or any other road to Mexico. In the process of trying to find an exit, I saw a government bus pull next to me. It was a school bus, painted white, with bars across the windows. It was, of course, some sort of transportation for detained persons, and it was headed straight south to the border.

Lots of faces looked out of those windows. I imagined that the passengers in that bus, however they had found themselves immigrating, were not experiencing the sort of joy we experience in Advent. Today, as we light this pink candle of joy, I think of those immigrants who were being returned across the border. While our spirits soar at the declaration of Christ's coming to us, they are travelling a less certain road.

I do not know, but I would assume that the passengers on that bus were immigrants being returned across the US/Mexico border. I assumed they were some of the thousands of immigrants and refugees who are returned to Mexico every month. My point is not to debate immigration policies, but to guide our attention to that bus and its precious cargo. It is easy to demonize those who risk their lives coming across the border. But in that moment, as I traveled down the freeway, I began to think about how their experience rubbed against my ideas of what it meant to find joy at Christmas.

I watched as the bus made its way toward the border. I thought of the words of our scripture lessons today. Isaiah also bears a word to those travelling along the highways of God. They, too, were immigrants searching for home. They were living lives filled with chaos and disruption, uncertainty and struggle. In that pain, Isaiah's words offer them glimmers of hope.

I also recalled the promises Jesus proclaimed in Matthew this morning. The gospel lesson evokes a similar experience of God's promises being spoken in a time of uncertainty and crisis. Jesus was confronted by the sorrowful disciples of John. He had been imprisoned, and they were unsure of what would happen next. Yet in this moment of uncertainty, Jesus delivered a promise of profound joy: While all the world may look bleak and uncertain, said Jesus, you go back to John and tell him what you have seen. Tell him of the promises you've heard, and the things that you have seen. Go and tell him that while the world is uncertain, this much is true: "The blind receive their sight, the lame walk, the lepers are cleansed, the deaf hear, the dead are raised, and the poor have good news brought to them." The kingdom is drawing near.

This is the promise which holds the possibility of true joy. It is an invitation extended to those who may have wandered among the ruins and wreckage of life. It is a call to see how hope is emerging, and an invitation to come home safely. For Isaiah, the promise is a call away from fear and grief, and invitation to find joy. He offers them the reminder of God's unmistakable presence that fills us with good things.

Likewise, Matthew reminded us, the messages of the prophets are guiding us to a deeper joy. We may have thought we were just experiencing some spectacle in the wilderness, but John's proclamation is preparing a new way toward joy.

On this third Sunday of Advent, we light the pink candle of joy — allowing its slender flames to peek out behind its purple siblings. On this Sunday, we recall the promise of joy. We join our voices with Mary, rejoicing at the promises of God which dance across the chasms of pain and struggle. Patting her growing belly, Mary managed to look beyond her bewildering circumstances to sing joyfully to God:

> My soul magnifies the Lord, and my spirit rejoices in God my Savior, for he has looked with favor on the lowliness of his servant. Surely, from now on all generations will call me blessed; for the mighty one has done great things for me" (Luke 2:46).

These are the words that invite us to find our joy. It's a joy not found in the glimmering tinsel and glitter of the season, but in the healing promises of a God who is with us in our stumbling and bumbling through life. These words bring comfort to the refugee, and hope to those filled with grief. Our God is coming to us, overthrowing the world's power plays by entering the world as a humble, helpless infant, whose birth brings deepest joy.

Here is our joy: God meets us on our journey. Even fools shall not go astray! Like Mary and Joseph, like the busload of immigrants, like mothers and fathers trying to get through the crazy weeks before Christmas, we are all on a journey.

Look at that candle. Some of our preschoolers call it "The Barbie Candle" because of its rosy-pink glow. It stands out against the other darker purple candles, perhaps as a reminder that the way the joy of Christmas enters our lives. That joy stands apart from the weary dreariness of the world, a reminder of the gift of God's peace.

As I flew home from that trip to California, the flight attendant tried to inject a little humor into the bland and well-rehearsed safety instructions we have all heard hundreds of times. He reminded us that the yellow vests under our seats would be useful in the rather unusual need of an emergency sea landing on the route between Denver and St. Louis. (Think about it). Then he reminded us of the oxygen masks and the appropriate way to put them on, adding, "For those of you travelling with young children… (he paused), why?" As we landed, he reminded us of the need for joy in this season and even quoted the book of Proverbs, "a merry heart makes a cheerful face."

He was trying to offer bits of lighthearted wisdom to weary travelers. Yet for those who have travelled the hardened highways of struggle and pain, there is the yearning for something more than smiling through our tears. John's disciples understood that joy comes even in times of grief, just as the prophet knew that those who had endured much pain need more than happy attitudes to find their deepest joy. Isaiah's words were spoken to people who had suffered and endured much pain. In our time, as well, the world is filled with the ravages of war and upheaval. At times, the wounds are visible, raw, and deep. It can feel as if there is no future, no possibility, and certainly no joy.

"When fear prevails in our hearts," wrote John Calvin, "we are as it were lifeless, so that we cannot raise even a finger to do anything; but when hope animates us, there is vigor in the whole body, so that alacrity appears everywhere."[12]

In the early days of the Ukrainian war, some in that country returned to their ruined cities only to face devastation. "I came here in case I could find anything to clean up a bit," one Ukrainian said as he returned to his home in Kamianka, Ukraine. "But there is nothing." [13] We resonate with that sort of emptiness, if only partially. We resonate with the emptiness felt by Ukrainians and Judeans not because we have experienced the waste of war, but because we have felt the blows of grief, the staggering defeats of loss, sadness and all sorts of other experiences that rob joy from us.

In the play and movie *August: Osage County*, a family grieving the loss of a father gathers for his funeral. The story of this family is one of dysfunction and pain: their mother was manipulative and mean, there were revelations of love triangles and affairs, and everyone was smoking and drinking too much. In the midst of this ugliness and despair one character said, "Thank God we can't know the future, or we'd never get out of bed."[14]

The promise God offers in Advent is that we are not left desolate or alone. By the flicker of the Advent candle of joy, we

12 Quoted by Jenifer Ryan Ayers, "Theological Perspective," *Feasting on the Word Advent Companion*.

13 See https://www.nytimes.com/2022/10/24/world/europe/ukraine-devastation-russian-retreat.html

14 Quoted in *Feasting on the Word: Advent Companion*, "Third Sunday of Advent," pastoral perspective by Deborah Block.

hear God's promise. We feel it deep within us. We listen to the joy of Mary and resonate with Isaiah's exultations: The desert and the dry land will be glad; the wilderness will rejoice and blossom like the crocus. They will burst into bloom and rejoice with joy and singing; they will receive the glory of Lebanon... strengthen the weak hands and support the unsteady knees. Say to those who are panicking: "Be strong! Don't fear! Here's your God!"

It is a word that breaks bonds of injustice, and a promise that brings us lasting hope. Isaiah pointed us toward our joy, even when the roads seemed impassable.

There is a story about an old man who lived alone on a farm he had worked for decades. One particularly icy winter, the man was forced to stay inside much of the winter. The pond on his farm was frozen over, and with every passing day of December, January, and February the layers of ice accumulated across the ground. It was too cold for the man to go outside and sit on the bench under his favorite apple tree. It was too cold to go anywhere, and by the time he would try to bundle up with layers of sweaters and scarves it was nearly too dark to go out anyway. Day after day, he would look outside the window and gaze upon every branch of his favorite apple tree.

But in his heart, the man trusted in a deeper promise. He trusted in the promise that the sun would melt the snow, that the ice would thaw, and that his favorite tree would one day bloom again. Even as the cold of winter lingered, he clung to this hope. And as spring arrived, he looked out and was filled with joy: the tree long covered in ice was beginning to be filled with buds.

This is the joy which floods our lives: we will drive along highways and never be lost, and we shall witness the blossoming of flowers in the deserts, and believe the joyful affirmation of Mary: truly, nothing shall be impossible for our God.

Amen.

The Days Are Hastening On

Be patient, therefore, beloved, until the coming of the Lord. The farmer waits for the precious crop from the earth, being patient with it until it receives the early and the late rains. You also must be patient. Strengthen your hearts, for the coming of the Lord is near. (v. 8)

Note:
Services of holiday remembrance and hope, sometimes referred to as "Blue Christmas," services or longest-night services are growing in popularity among churches. Though not included in the Revised Common Lectionary, these services are frequently held on or near the date of the winter solstice. On this day, the northern hemisphere is tilted away from the sun, creating the longest night of the calendar year. Congregations have found that "Blue Christmas" services can be occasions for reaching out to those who are grieving or who may be experiencing a different type of Christmas. Our congregation normally sends special invitations to those who have experienced losses, inviting them to come and share in a time of reflection and worship. This meditation draws on the Epistle reading for the Third Sunday of Advent.

One year, an unseasonably warm week before Thanksgiving prompted more than a few in our neighborhood to get an early start putting up their Christmas lights. I'm not even sure if the week before Thanksgiving counts as early anymore! There were a fair number of houses which seemed to switch seamlessly from Halloween straight to Christmas. It left a few of us wondering what to do with the Valentine's Day wreaths which were still on our front doors.

Advent can feel like that: someone turns a switch and *SWOOSH* we move from Trick-or-Treat to Santa, from the relaxed, pumpkin-spiced days of autumn to the breakneck pace of Christmas. There is a race to be the first one to plug in your lights, to be the first to send cards, to wrap packages, to bake cookies and to mark off all the other items on your holiday bingo card. For lo, as the carol goes, the days are hastening on — and so are we.

Yet the holiday spin cycle can often feel as if life's crushing load has fallen on us. That is especially true for those who are grieving, or who are experiencing a different sort of holiday. Perhaps there is an empty place in our hearts or around our holiday tables this year. Or perhaps our memories of Christmas are just too much for us. "I'm just not feeling it this year," someone said to me, and I understood what she meant.

It is exactly for that reason that each year, when the night is longest, we take a breath. We take a moment to pause and to remember, honoring the many different emotions and feelings that we may be experiencing. We take time to listen for a word of hope, and dare to name the grief inside of us.

"Blue Christmas" is not a time to sing like Elvis, but a time to recall that while many see bright lights of gold, red, and green, some see only blue. We are near to the winter solstice, the time of the longest night of the year. Still, we dare to recall that there is a Light shining in the darkness. Blair Gilmer Meeks reminds us that "in this season when we are expecting the joy of Christ's coming…we know that for some members of our community every night appears endless and the prospect of a new day seems dim."[15]

"Be patient," urged the writer of James. His words come to us as an assurance to rejoice even in moments when joy is hard to find. If we are honest, that is how many of us who are

---

15 Blair Gilmer Meeks, *Season of Light and Hope*, (Nashville, TN: Abingdon Press, 2005), p. 48.

grieving feel this year. Caught in the vice grip of complicated Christmas emotions, we may find it hard to wait for the day of the Lord.

As I look at the way the world rushes toward Christmas, I often wonder: "What, exactly, is the hurry?" Are we trying to embrace memories of a presumed joy and happiness that elude us? Are we hoping to rekindle feelings of closeness to loved ones that we have lost, only to be disappointed when our experiences never match that ideal? Perhaps we speed up the holidays because of the rush of holiday endorphins inflating us with feelings of joy—just like those inflatable Snoopies and Santa Clauses that pop up around our neighborhoods every night.

But drive around those same neighborhoods early the next morning. All you see are deflated skins lying lifeless on the ground. In similar fashion, when our lives become hooked on the sped-up Christmas, we find ourselves so quickly depleted, disappointed, and empty.

In this secular age, as theologian Andrew Root argues, "time itself has been emptied of the sacred."[16] He is writing about the church and Christians in a secular time. Too often, he argues, the church accedes to this notion of secular time. In doing so, we trade our mission of pondering God's time for an ever-moving machine that does nothing but grind up our souls and scatter them like trash.

Advent calls us away from such weariness. Advent is an act of resistance to the cultural hyper-speed of Christmas. Instead of rushing, we're invited to a holy patience grounded in hope. James uses an agricultural metaphor: a farmer plants his crops and waits with eager expectation, knowing that the work of growing is happening in secret, hidden beneath the soil.

While we may hope that the lights of Christmas will brighten our lives, the reality is that we often awaken feeling as deflated as our neighbor's blow-up sleigh and reindeer when the

---

16 Andrew Root, *The Congregation in a Secular Age*, (Ada, MI: Baker Academic Press, 2021), p. 53.

power gets turned off. Instead of plunging into that weariness, we are called instead to the sort of honesty with ourselves found so often in the recovery community. Advent seems to function much like those first steps offered by Alcoholics Anonymous: "we admitted we were powerless over alcohol — our lives had become unmanageable."

Instead, we come to light candles. We resist the push and pull of mindlessly scurrying around. Instead, we brace ourselves for the startling honest words of the prophets. We lean into the promise that because our God will come to us, we can be patient. James' farming images are compelling, even if we've never lived anywhere near agriculture. The hope of Christ calls us to a life of cultivating patience.

We trust in God's promises, even though letting the seeds of patience germinate can feel interminable. If we don't, we trade these promises for a sped-up version of life that squeezes every ounce of joy and peace from us like a kid grabbing a tube of toothpaste. Speeding up our lives inevitably leads to the sort of crises decried by the Hebrew prophets. Burdens are placed on the poor, offerings given out of obligation and not generosity. Injustices are done to the orphan and the widow, and violence devours our lives and land.

In response, we are offered the reminder that patience can be restorative. We trade the message of immediacy — "in these days," — for words of lasting hope. Indeed, the days are hastening on, and we are too. For in those coming days, a child shall be born. In those days magi shall appear, in those days John the Baptist shall appear in the wilderness, in those days the promises of God shall come to us.

In days to come, we will move beyond the darkness of this night into a hope that shall last. Candles will be lit, and carols sung. In the days to come, kids will put on their dad's bathrobes and be transformed into royal wise persons. In days to come, our ordinary moments will be graced by sacred time.

Andy Root suggested that the church might consider how sacred time can be marked by encounters with God and with each other. In these deep Advent encounters we sense something new is happening. Our feelings of constant fatigue and emptiness are replaced with hope.

Hope in the days to come. Hope that comes from the light of a single candle. Hope that emerges from knowing we are loved not because of our accomplishments or achievements, but simply because we are valued by God. Hope that violence ends by turning weapons into gardening tools.

As Edmund Sears reminded us in his classic carol "It Came Upon a Midnight Clear:"

> And ye, beneath life's crushing load,
> whose forms are bending low,
> who toil along the climbing way
> with painful steps and slow,
> look now! for glad and golden hours
> come swiftly on the wing.
> O rest beside the weary road,
> and hear the angels sing![17]

These are the real words for our Christmas countdown. Amen.

---

17 Edmund H. Sears, *"It Came Upon A Midnight Clear,"* (1849).

Joseph's Decision

When (Jesus') mother Mary had been engaged to Joseph,
but before they lived together, she was found to be preg-
nant from the Holy Spirit. Her husband Joseph, being a
righteous man and unwilling to expose her to public dis-
grace, planned to divorce her quietly… (Matthew 1:18)

If you have ever had the responsibility for casting a church
Sunday school Christmas pageant, then you know that the
hardest part to cast is always Joseph. We have had a wide va-
riety of Josephs over the years, including at least one who was
technically more "Josephina" than Joseph. We have had the
young Josephs who were filled with wide-eyed enthusiasm,
nearly giddy with Christmas joy and filled with paternal pride.
We have had the few who were reluctant to have been asked,
but who nonetheless rose to the occasion, especially when
they were bribed with a plate of homemade Christmas cookies. Others, perhaps even a slim majority, were either terrified
or present only under extreme duress. At times some of them
seemed to be like prisoners of war, held captive by the enemy
and appearing only under threat of severe repercussions from
their mothers.

But when bribes fail, more than one of them have been in-
voluntarily conscripted for the role. Once a staff member cor-
nered her eighth-grade son. He was summarily grabbed by the
scruff of his neck and plopped in the manger shortly before
the pageant began. And then there was another completely less
than enthusiastic Joseph who stood as far away from Mary as
possible, looking a bit like Robert DeNiro in "The Deer Hunter."

In the classic story "The Best Christmas Pageant Ever," children's author Barbara Robinson captured some of this ambivalence about Joseph. The story, you may recall, was about an unruly family of juvenile delinquents who take over a church's Christmas pageant one year. The Herdman children were described as wild and undisciplined kids who always appeared disheveled and one step away from juvenile hall. They had never shown any interest in church until they learn that the Sunday school served snacks after the lesson. They showed up and suddenly took an interest in the Christmas pageant, grabbing all the parts they could.

As Robinson wrote, the Herdman's collective jaws dropped and they sat straight up in their seats as the Sunday school teacher read them the story of Jesus' birth. Since the Herdman family had never heard the story of Jesus' birth, the Sunday school teacher read it to them from the Bible. "This was a pain in the neck to most of us because we knew the whole thing backward and forward and never had to be told anything except who were supposed to be, and where we were supposed to stand," says the narrator. As the teacher continues reading, "...Joseph and Mary, his espoused wife, being great with child," Ralph Herdman — who had volunteered to be Joseph — blurted out: "Pregnant!"

"Well," the narrator continues, "That stirred things up. All the big kids began to giggle, and all the little kids wanted to know what was so funny, and the teacher had to hammer the floor with a blackboard pointer. "That's enough, Ralph," she said, and continued the story.[18]

We can laugh at these nativity tropes, but there is a bit of truth in these accounts. The scandalous truth is that even the gospel writers do not know what to do about Joseph, and frankly we have typically not understood completely his sacrifice and decision.

---

18 Barbara Robinson, *The Best Christmas Pageant Ever*, (HarperCollins Reprint Edition, 2011).

His appearances in the New Testament are brief — neither Paul nor Mark mentioned Joseph at all, while John only alluded to him. It is only Matthew who provides us with any semblance of a sketch about Joseph. The fact of the matter is that while Mary is shining in the spotlight, Joseph is in the shadows. He got, as one of my friends said recently, a relatively short shrift in the whole Christmas story.

If we are at all truthful about Joseph, then Ralph Herdman's startled expletive might be as accurate as anything we know about Jesus' earthly father. Joseph entered the story not as the strong silent type, but as someone who found himself in a morally conflicted situation, anxious, uncertain, and timid at best. And, I believe, that in telling this truthful story of Joseph we discover a profound truth about faith: *our choices to follow God are nearly always moments of quiet courage.*

Quiet courage, notes Gil Rendle, is the decision to move forward when no one knows what to do. Quiet courage offers no memorable words or persuasive arguments. It is not the result of a motivational speech, good coaching or careful strategy. It is, instead, a purposeful movement forward that is always risky. As Rendle writes, "While others argue about the right way to do things, quiet courage stepped up to fulfill the intended purpose of the moment." [19] He continues — leaders, he insisted, must change from merely being good leaders to engaging in quiet, courageous, and purposeful leadership.

Joseph's story is a story for all of us. It is a story of quiet courage that looks beyond the obstacles, and trusts that God is greater than all our plans.

The nineteenth-century French painter James Tissot may have captured the most compelling image of Joseph. You may wish to see an image of the painting at the Brooklyn Museum of Art website. What we see in Tissot's portrait — aptly

19 Gil Rendle, *Quietly Courageous*, (Lanham, MD: Rowman and Littlefield Publishing, 2019).

named the "Anxiety of St. Joseph,"[20] is a man who faces a confusing and bewildering world. All of what he has known about the world has evaporated. This is not the life he had planned. Mary's confusing, unexpected circumstances leave him anxious and worried.

I've always imagined that it would be helpful if we had Joseph's testimony recorded verbatim, but there appears to be no transcript available. If Herod convened a special committee to investigate the birth of the "one called the King of the Jews," no one bothered to hire a stenographer. I can imagine the stir in the crowd as the high priests call their first witness: Joseph, of Nazareth, son of David, an otherwise model citizen who tries his best to stay under the radar.

"Joseph, please, be seated. Now, we're not trying to intimidate you, though please remember we can throw you and your family into jail. We just want to get a few details straight. Tell, us please, your name and occupation for the record."

"I am Joseph, of Nazareth, a descendent of King David, a carpenter."

"You are a descendent of David? A poor carpenter from that backwater village? How can we be sure?"

"Well, sir, I've got it written here in the family Bible. "Abraham begat Isaac; and Isaac begat Jacob; and Jacob begat Judas and his brethren; And Judas begat Phares and Zara of Thamar; and Phares begat Esrom; and Esrom begat Aram; And Aram begat Aminadab; and Aminadab begat Naasson; and Naasson begat Salmon; And Salmon begat Booz of Rachab; and Booz begat Obed of Ruth; and Obed begat Jesse; And Jesse begat David the king; and David the king begat Solomon of her that had been the wife of Urias; And Solomon begat Roboam; and Roboam begat Abia; and Abia begat Asa; and…"

"Yes, yes, yes, I get it. You are of the house and lineage of David."

---

20 See "The Anxiety of Joseph" (L'Anxiete de Saint Joseph), by James Tissot, (1886-1894), found at https://www.brooklynmuseum.org/opencollection/objects/4426, accessed 9/26/2024.

"Yes, sir."

"And your wife is Mary."

"Yes, sir."

"And she is great with child, and you have already announced that it is a boy, and you will name him Jesus?"

"Yes, that's right."

"How did you pick the name of Jesus?"

"That's what the angel told me."

"Oh, yes, the angel. Did you ring a bell for this angel?"

"No, sir, of course not. The angel appeared to me in a dream."

"Oh, a dream? So does this happen often — angels talking to you in your dreams?"

"Well, not until recently."

"And what else did the angel say to you, Joseph?"

"The angel told me to not be afraid. Now, don't get me wrong, that's what angels always say, because if there is anything that is going to make you afraid, it is an angel speaking to you in a dream. But anyway, the angel's words conveyed a certain confidence to me."

"Confidence? Why should you, a carpenter, living quietly in Nazareth be afraid?"

"It was because Mary was pregnant. And I knew I wasn't the father."

"You knew you were not the father?"

"Yes, that's right." (The commissioners shake in their seats as reporters whisper to themselves. "Joseph, do you know what happens to a woman who is unfaithful to her husband?"

"Of course. The commandments, the law, is clear: she is to be put aside. Sometimes she is to be punished with death. I know the commandments."

"But you did not do this?" "At first, I was content to seek a quick divorce — I thought maybe we could to Jerusalem and get one of those $99 quickie divorces. But then I had the dream."

"That's when the angel spoke to you. And to be clear, the angel said, 'Do not be afraid?'"

"Yes, that's correct. What I learned is that God had a purpose I never understood. If I may, your honors, what I would like to say to you is that what I first thought was bad news was actually very good news. Someone told me to think about it this way: "What appears to be a moral outrage is, in fact, a holy disruption. The child is Mary's womb is not a violation of God's will, but an expression of it, a gift from the Holy Spirit."[21] You see, the angel told me that Jesus would save his people from their sins."

At this, the hearing room explodes with cries of shock and horror. "Blasphemy! This man should be taken away! Only God can forgive sins!"

And suddenly, right in that hearing, Joseph slips away. The courtroom is filled with terror, shock, worry. The high priests adjourn the meeting and order the room to be emptied. No one is quite certain what to think.

Joseph, meanwhile, knows the truth. Joseph knows the real scandal that has happened. He has remained faithful, always attentive to where God is at work in the world. He has listened—not only to his anxiety, but to something deeper, something within him that fills him with peace. In the face of the unbearable, harsh, and frightening truth, the pulse beating within Mary's womb is a reminder God will be with us. He has taken the risk and has found that the promise of God is true: that the risk of listening to God is the only things which matters.

Amen.

---

21 Thomas Long, Matthew, p. 13.

Pondering Matters

So they went with haste and found Mary and Joseph and the child lying in the manger. When they saw this, they made known what had been told them about this child, and all who heard it were amazed at what the shepherds told them, and Mary treasured all these words and pondered them in her heart (Luke 2:16-19).

Let's take a cue from Mary this Christmas. Instead of counting the bills or fretting over menus, take a moment to join her in pondering what had just happened. The nativity was a spiritually rich moment, packed with sweetness and poignancy, which may help us remember that pondering is much more than trying to recall where Santa put the extra batteries.

Let us take a breath and join her in an act of holy remembering.

Most Christmas mornings offer little room for reflecting on the meaning of the moment. We are completely focused on the moment, and perhaps that is as it should be. We throw ourselves into packages, perhaps only coming up for air to look for batteries or more coffee. Some Christmases we rush through everything so fast that we forget which gift came from whom, which always makes for awkward phone calls later in the day!

This is why pondering matters.

With Mary, we need to find some sort of foothold in the careening chaos of Christmas. She stops to breathe and to think, imagining how the child that has been born will make a difference. Luke has given us a couple of clues: we understand that the incarnation reaffirms God's desire to work with the powerless and poor. We know that Mary sees the connections between the shimmering glory of God and the utter foolishness of the emperor.

Luke's narrative moved us this far, following the stages of Mary's pregnancy to her delivery. The star shone high above the city, guiding shepherds and others to the place where Jesus had been born. God had entered the world not through the doors of a palace, but the side doors of a barn. That alone is sufficient fodder for pondering.

But we make pondering ponderous. To ponder means to think carefully about something. Meanwhile, "ponderous" means clumsy or "oppressively or unpleasantly dull." (That's nearly the same language my children used to describe my sermons when they were younger.) Luke's story of Jesus' nativity is an invitation to join Mary an act of holy remembrance. Clutching Jesus, she cradles the multivalent memories of his birth.

Parents treasure those first moments of their child's life. My wife and I have distinct memories of each of our children's births, and I'm sure that my memories are not quite as clear as hers! Our eldest was delivered by C-section after long hours of non-productive labor. It happened that my wife's doctor was a friend of ours. As Carol was being wheeled into the operating room, Doug led me to the scrub sink. A nurse put a gown on me and covered my hair before I entered the OR. Stepping into the surgical suite filled me with a fanboy-like amazement. Having never missed a single episode of 1980s medical dramas like *E/R*, I was fascinated by wife's medical team. "You should see what they are doing to you," I said to my wife. No, she should not have. Our friend immediately reprimanded me and told me to sit down and pay attention to the one person who mattered…my wife, the soon-to-be mother.

We don't know what Mary pondered that evening, but I'm sure she never forgot the look on Joseph's face! Imagine Mary holding Jesus close, counting ten fingers and ten toes, wiping away the remnants of birth, allowing his skin to touch hers. The miracle of all miracles had occurred: God in human flesh appeared.

Think of how this birth story intersects our own journeys, suffusing our struggles and pain with treasures of grace and truth. Mary invites us to a time of holy wondering, of imagining just how the holy will come to dwell among ordinary humans. Ponder the ways God continues to show up in this world, full of grace and truth. Take a breath and ponder anew what Christmas means. Share these stories of grace, confident God is at work.

Ponder what it means for us to be like the shepherds—witnesses to the boldness of God in flesh appearing. Where the world wants to flatten experiences of delight and mystery into easily digestible chunks, Jesus' birth gives us reason to explore the mystery of it all.

We confuse this work of recollection, often assuming pondering is the same as ponderous. But, as Mother Mary taught, pondering is likely the most significant gift we can receive. This was what Luke called us to remember.

This familiar story becomes new to us as we heed Luke's invitation to enter that makeshift birthing suite. As you notice the surroundings, see if you can hear the crowds out in the streets. Check out the surprised faces of the shepherds as they make their awkward entrance. Clad in clothes that reeked of sheep dung and earthy smells, they were hardly the sort of attendants you'd invite into a labor and delivery room. But still their unshaven faces were filled with signs of the glory of God.

Here in this place, she sensed how the holy moved closer to dwell with the ordinary. That was the power of that moment. As Mary embraced her child, she thought of how the thoughts of the proud have been scattered. She discovered the grace of a child entering the world in the ordinary way, but with a most exceptional purpose. No wonder she sang of God lifting the lowly and filling the hungry with good things.

I wonder if Mary pondered how the holiness of this moment would soon permeate the world, saturating it with amazement and hope. Jesus wriggled and cried, and then cooed and was calm. The world has long awaited his arrival. Mary curiously considered the messages that had been shared with her: the angel who promised she had found favor with God; her cousin who called her blessed; the smelly shepherds who had seen the hosts of heaven. By the tender mercies of God, all this had happened, coming to us "to give light to those who sit in darkness and in the shadow of death, to guide our feet into the way of peace" (Luke 1:78-79).

So let us ponder this thing that has happened. Let it fill us with sanctified amazement. To see the holy dwelling in an ordinary, ramshackle manger is indeed astonishing. It defied expectations and changed the course of the world.

"This is thy hour, O Soul," wrote Walt Whitman. "Thy free flight into the wordless…" His friend and mentor Ralph Waldo Emerson commented on this short poem by saying, "Here we find ourselves suddenly, if not in a critical speculation, but in a holy place, and should go warily and reverently."[22]

Go, and ponder what it means to be guided from this holy place into a world yearning for signs of God's love.

I read once that Newtown, Connecticut, the site of the horrendous shootings at Sandy Hook Elementary School in December, 2012, has been called both a "cradle of grief," and also a place of "untold love and quiet resilience."[23] It is a stinging memory, and an unhealed wound aggravated each time another school shooting happens.

But pondering that "cradle of grief" and the birthstool of "quiet resilience" may refresh us with not only the memories of those who died and who survived, but also with the steadfast hope of Mary. We ponder not only the desperate sadness of our world, but also the promise that nothing is impossible for the Lord. As the holy invites us to dance, we ponder the possibilities.

22 Walt Whitman, "A Clear Midnight," (1881), accessed at https://poets.org/poem/clear-midnight 9/26/2024.

23 "Ten years after Sandy Hook, the victims memories still endure," December 14, 2022, https://www.cnn.com/2022/12/14/us/sandy-hook-newtown-shooting-victims-profiles/index.html.

Our human hearts may be weighed down, but in this moment, we also know that Mary's heart captured a glimpse of God's glory. It was not much, but it was sufficient...and it gave Mary enough to ponder all these things that happened.

Amen.

The Dreams We Have For Children

Now after they had left, an angel of the Lord appeared to Joseph in a dream and said, "Get up, take the child and his mother, and flee to Egypt, and remain there until I tell you, for Herod is about to search for the child, to destroy him." (v. 13)

Joseph's dreams had the habit of becoming living nightmares. I imagine him waking up in the middle of the night, sweat pouring from his brow. Mary looked at him and shook her sleepy head. "Another dream?" she asked tentatively. "Maybe I need to lay off the garlic," he said, struggling to pull the covers up to his face. The struggle was real.

As Matthew recounted Joseph's story, Joseph hardly got a good night's sleep. While Joseph said little, his dreams evoked mixtures of dread and excitement. It was one thing to learn you're going to become a foster father to God's Son, but perhaps quite another to discover the empire had put a target on your back.

This time the angel even skipped the serene salutation. The customary angelic assurance of "Be not afraid" was bypassed in favor of an urgent message: Herod is out to get your child. It was an alarming, even traumatizing message. The child was in danger, and there was no time to waste.

A friend who had been a pastor in Cuba once shared with me how he and his wife developed a plan to emigrate to the United States. They would trade hushed whispers late at night, long after their children had gone asleep. A secret plan emerged, along with the unexpressed fears of what might happen if the plan fell apart.

These are the whispers Joseph heard. The angel was not bringing good news of great joy, but was instead summoning Joseph to a deeper obedience. "Get up, take the child and his mother, and flee to Egypt," the angel warned. Life as a refugee was better than waiting to be killed, but the angel's message eroded any hope that Mary and Joseph might enjoy a few years of normal family life. Joseph's dreams suddenly became a nightmare.

On the second Sunday of Christmas, this text seems almost too traumatizing to preach. Bible scholar Kenneth Bailey once wrote that for him, Herod's assault on innocent children was one story that should never be told on television.[24] Herod's brutality was fed by his narcissistic paranoia, his reign characterized by the knowledge that he was never fully embraced by the people he ruled nor fully accepted by the emperor he served.

The angel's announcement to Joseph was a reminder that under Herod, no one was safe. Soon blood would flow through the streets of Judea, a poignant reminder of the empire's tyrannical power. No babies would be safe, and one can only imagine the trauma that was inflicted on an entire generation.

Joseph and Mary hightailed it out of town, with the sweet-smell of frankincense and myrrh trailing behind them. Yet the cost of Jesus' arrival remained steep.

This is not the stuff of Christmas plays and pageants. Herod slaughtered the children of his own subjects, a chilling reminder of the way the empire did indeed strike back against the promises of God. Joseph's dreams underscored the unfolding promises of the incarnation as a sign of God's presence with those who suffered.

His nightmares sound familiar to parents, and indeed are echoed throughout our culture. The Catholic church continues to reverberate from the ongoing "tsunami" of reported cases

---

24 Kenneth Bailey, *Jesus Through Middle Eastern Eyes* (Downers Grove, IL: Inter-Varsity Press, 2008), p. 56.

of child sexual abuse,[25] including from countries where allegations have never been made before.

Yet abuse is not restricted to churches. Journalists reviewing America's broken foster care system have found that states often spend more money removing children from homes than helping to reunite and stabilize families. Even worse, reports indicate that race and poverty are often factors in determining how children are removed from their families. An attorney interviewed by the Kansas City Star newspaper noted that "families are more often ripped apart for poverty and not abuse."[26]

As the sounds of Rachel's inconsolable cries rose above the Christmas din, so did the promises of one child, sheltered by caring hands who dared to trust in God's dream. For many children, however, that dream will always be a nightmare. Their lives and their bodies will be forever marked by trauma.

Matthew scholar Warren Carter aptly captured the evil intent of Herod's rage by calling these verses "The Empire Strikes Back."[27] Herod peeled back the golden-tinted veneer of Jesus' birth, reminding us that this family remained vulnerable and at risk. Yet Matthew asserted that this helpless, vulnerable infant remained the true king of the Jews. His rule stood opposed to the would-be king, as Matthew demonstrated in his genealogical account of Jesus' origins in chapter one.

Herod understood the political threat posed by the child. What he did not understand was that his usual tactics were futile against the power of God. His frightened and anxious response would not prevent God's plan. His fury at the magi's deception fueled his determined response to contain the child at all costs.

---

25 See https://apnews.com/article/the-reckoning-ap-top-news-international-news-sexual-abuse-by-clergy-europe-6e99b1ddf64d5fd7ff85fe065d-699e7b, accessed 12/19/2024.

26 See: https://www.kansascity.com/news/special-reports/article238243099.html, accessed 12/19/2024.

27 Warren Carter, *Matthew and the Margins*, p. 73.

Despite Herod's paranoia, God remained firmly in control. Herod would be no match for the subversive resistance of God—just as Pharoah was no match against the people of Israel. The empire's control was an illusion. Yet the pain created by that empire was not imaginary. Even a rogue despot can cause mayhem, as the insurance commercials regularly remind us. Enraged, Herod ordered the massacre of children, while the hunted one escaped. Eventually it would be that child who triumphed over the powers of the empire by declaring that "all authority and power" had been given to him.

There are lots of theological questions to be unpacked, of course. One wonders how traumatic memories and potential survivor's guilt remained with Mary, Joseph, and yes, Jesus. The accounts offer no easy answers, but instead point to the wider purposes of God. For now, however, the child was under the protective care of his earthly foster father. Joseph received the dream and embraced his role, even if he did not fully understand what was at stake.

All of that makes this story tough to preach and hard to accept. This week's text is hardly the stuff of Christmas pageants. Matthew takes us beyond the merriment of the season by reminding his readers that while the Lord of lords had been born; he remained a threat to the empires of this world.

It took a dream to keep him safe. Actually, it took a couple: one to the "wise guys," to warn them not to play into Herod's hand, and another to Joseph to once again follow God's leading. There is little about this story that can be included in sweet and sentimental holiday cards — anymore than if we included the faces of the millions of refugee and immigrant children who are at risk today. It is, scholars remind us, the very vulnerability of Jesus that underscored Matthew's message. The gospel is a story of a God who is truly Emmanuel — God *with* us.

In keeping with the dream motif, let's imagine what our congregation's dreams for children might be this year. But instead of dreaming of Sunday school rooms filled every week with children eagerly listening to Bible lessons, what would happen if we dared to dream a bit differently? How might our dreams of children include those who have been abused, maligned, or marginalized?

Instead of running away from this sharp-edged text, let us allow the message of Emmanuel to remain with us in these often-dreary days of January. Perhaps our dreams of a perfect Christmas were not realized, but that does not mean the dream of God is over.

Jesus' body carried the laments of Rachel's tearful cries, as well as the cries of hundreds of other parents who watched their children be consumed by an angry, relentless dictator. Today the church must dare to dream on behalf of wounded children and embody the sort of faithfulness chosen by Joseph. Those are the dreams we must have for children. May it be so.

Amen.

When The Holy And Ordinary Dance

"But the angel said to them, "Do not be afraid, for see, I am bringing you good news of great joy for all the people: to you is born this day in the city of David a Savior, who is the Messiah, the Lord…When the eighth day came, it was time to circumcise the child, and he was called Jesus, the name given by the angel before he was conceived in the womb.(Luke 2:15, 21)

A couple of years ago, the planets Jupiter and Saturn were in alignment in an event that astronomers called the "Great Conjunction." I always thought "so and yet" were the great conjunctions, but that's because I was a journalism major and avoided astronomy classes like the plague.

Scientists reported that this "Great Conjunction" had not happened since March 4, 1226. I wonder how they knew that, especially since cable news channels had yet to be a thing. Some astrologers had gone so far to say they believed the alignment of the two planets may have been the "Star of Bethlehem" which led the magi on their search for the baby Jesus.

It was a marvelous sight — two planets, millions of miles away, yet aligned so beautifully that we could see them from our front yard. This conjunction brought to my mind the lovely Christmas anthem by Robert C. Lau: "Cool night, quiet night, candle light…heaven's light."[28]

The star of Bethlehem shines bright around us, leading us to another astonishing conjunction: the aligning of God with

28 Robert C. Lau, *Cool Night, Quiet Night*, Lorenz Publishing Company (1994).

us. We recall the greatest conjunction as we retell that old and familiar story. Lights dancing in the eyes of sheep, glimmers of the angelic host declaring God's praise to befuddled shepherds. A young couple summoned by imperial authorities to participate in a census. They are far from home, unattended by the modern accoutrements of hospital birthing suites. The time came for Mary to be delivered, and like any first-time parents, there was plenty of anxiety and worry to go around.

Painful twangs of labor pushed Mary into the ground. The night wind was blowing, and only Joseph was there to witness the birth of their son. It was a cool, quiet night and in the heavens, an announcement of something astonishing: the holy had come to dance with ordinary shepherds and anxious parents. We hear the first announcement of the child's name: "Savior, the Messiah...the Lord."

It is the only time in the New Testament when these three titles appear together. The frightened shepherds, working class folk so vital to the economy yet also equally despised and marginalized were the ones to whom this holy announcement was made. Yet the terms "Savior," and "Messiah," "Lord" also carry important, if not regal significance. The announcement was imbued with religious and political meaning: the child was to be considered nothing less than a liberator sent to redeem a people who were oppressed.[29]

It was the official announcement, the proclamation of God's Son appearing in human flesh.

Days later, after the shepherds had gone home, the baby has been cleaned, and the casseroles eaten, Mary and Joseph present their child in the Temple, fulfilling the obligations of their faith. He is circumcised according to the Law of Moses, and once more he is named. Yet this time he is called Jesus, a form of Joshua. It is the name disclosed to Mary and Joseph, a name they carry on their hearts. An ordinary name, but in the

29 Justo L. González, Luke, ed. Amy Plantinga Pauw and William C. Placher, Belief: A Theological Commentary on the Bible (Louisville, KY: Westminster John Knox Press, 2010), p. 36.

great conjunction of God's providence, a name joined to the holiness of the incarnation.

The story is as simple as that, yet because it is so familiar to us, we tend to dress it up a bit. We add romantic flourishes and do our best to make it worthy of a Christmas pageant. After all, what's so exciting about a homeless couple giving birth? We jazz up the story a bit with imaginative details and characters. We add donkeys and an arrogant and cruel inn keeper. We speed up the magi's arrival time and even upgrade them to royalty status. We crowd the manger with shepherds and sheep. And, in some versions, just as Mary was about to put the child to sleep, we insert a teenage boy who thinks now would be a great time for a percussion solo.

We resist thinking about the birth of Jesus in its rawest and most rough reality. A few years ago, a church in California made national headlines because it portrayed the Nativity Scene as an immigrant family kept behind barbed wire and chained link. It's not a version we care to embrace. Instead, we make the Holy Family into a spectacle instead of seeing them in their astonishing and unpolished reality. And when we do that, we miss the mystery of what is happening: God slipping into our world almost unnoticed. The moment is itself a wondrous conjunction — the joining of the holy into the ordinary, the pairing of God and humanity, the sacred aligning with the everyday.

As familiar as we are with this story, let us not miss its power to challenge and transform us. Scholar Stephen Carlson has suggested that our image of Mary giving birth in a stable may not quite match the meaning of the original Greek word. Luke may not have been suggesting an overcrowded hotel but instead a room that was large enough for a husband and wife but not suitable for giving birth. Carlson went on to imagine this holy scene taking place in the midst of a larger common room — a place filled with all of Joseph's relatives who remained present during the dangers and perils of childbirth. Now it may not give you comfort to think that Joseph's Cousin

Eddy was offering color commentary on Mary's labor process, but what Carlson was aiming at was a reminder that this birth was more ordinary than it was spectacular.

From the very start, this king would be forever connected to the people he came to serve. He was not a king tucked away in the comfort of a fortress, but a child plucked straight into the vulnerability and vagaries of ordinary human life. The holy and the sacred lie mingled in the manger of Bethlehem, attended to by shepherds and later surrounded by the symbols of their ancient faith.

That is our good news. It is the good news of all the years, of course, but it is especially good news for those of us who have experienced the brutality of oppressive viruses, unrelenting terrorism, and political vengeance. Not unlike Mary and Joseph, we understand a bit about how the brutal realities can upend our lives, leaving us disconnected. In November 2021, my wife contracted Covid-19. Her condition plummeted quickly, and I soon found myself dropping her off at the emergency room. She climbed into a wheelchair, and I pushed her toward the entrance, which was as far as I was allowed to go. The nurse told me "We'll take good care of her," but like Mary looking at her newborn, I wondered. Immediately my wife and I were disconnected. As hospital's door slid shut, we experienced the brutality of disconnection. Oh, how we needed a Savior…a Messiah…a Lord.

When she returned home two weeks later, she was weak, but we were grateful. She had survived, thanks to good medicine and outstanding nurses and doctors. They mediated God's grace…and in their ordinary, human hands, we saw evidence of that great joining together of the holy and the ordinary. We saw not only the greatness of God's salvation, but the ways it came to us in the lives of ordinary people like a nurse named Deb, a doctor named Tom, and countless others.

God came to us, heralded as Messiah, Savior, and Lord. But he also arrived in our brokenness, cuddled in our arms, and we call him Jesus. His birth was announced with the host of heaven proclaiming, "Do not be afraid!"

God is with us: that is the stunning good news which the shepherds hear, and which Mary feels deep within her. The announcement of that good news meant that holiness and ordinariness shall dance together, that God had entered our universe. We did not, and do not, need to be afraid.

It is the joining of the holiness of God with the ordinariness of human life that fills this story of power. Jesus was Emmanuel, God with us. He was born into our anxious, fearful-world. He knew the pain we experience, and the ugliness of betrayal. He challenges us to see God's grace lifting us from despair. Thanks be to God!

Amen.

New Year's Day

Matthew 25:31-46

Training Our Eyes

"When the Son of Man comes in his glory and all the angels with him, then he will sit on the throne of his glory. All the nations will be gathered before him, and he will separate people one from another as a shepherd separates the sheep from the goats, and he will put the sheep at his right hand and the goats at the left. Then the king will say to those at his right hand, 'Come, you who are blessed by my Father, inherit the kingdom prepared for you from the foundation of the world, for I was hungry and you gave me food, I was thirsty and you gave me something to drink, I was a stranger and you welcomed me, I was naked and you gave me clothing, I was sick and you took care of me, I was in prison and you visited me.' Then the righteous will answer him, 'Lord, when was it that we saw you hungry and gave you food or thirsty and gave you something to drink? (vv. 31-39)

For several of my high school years, the week between Christmas and New Year's was spent inside chilly warehouses not far from Pasadena, California. Our church youth group had managed to snag a chance to earn money by helping decorate Rose Parade floats. Our little youth group worked twelve hours — sometimes longer — pushing petals, seeds, and other sorts of organic materials onto the large floats for the famed parade. As I remember, our labors earned the church a $1,000 donation. In 1979, that sounded like a lot of money.

In reality, it was a paltry sum paid by big corporations that were spending tens of thousands of dollars to have their product advertised on national television. One year we worked on the float of a well-known Japanese automobile manufacturer. Other years were spent decorating displays of a popular soft drink. (In addition to the $1,000, that company provided us with *unlimited* hot and cold samples of its famous soda, which is probably why I'm strictly a Diet Coke guy today.)

According to the Rose parade organizers, every inch of these magnificently designed floats must be covered with organic materials—usually flowers, but also seeds, leaves, bark, and so on. While we assumed we'd be pushing roses into the sides of the display, that was a job reserved for professional decorators.

Youth volunteers were given the harder, and certainly less fulfilling jobs, of gluing seeds and other stuff to the frame. What had sounded so glamorous was quickly reduced to grunt work that few teenagers enjoyed. Sometimes we would work for hours getting a certain material to stick, only to have one of the decorators decide it all had to be ripped apart and replaced with something different. Apparently, their eyes could see things ours could not.

When parade day would roll around, we'd gather at someone's house to watch for our float. Normally these behemoths don't make it far down Colorado Boulevard until they break down, but as long as they start the parade they remain eligible for prizes. After waiting and waiting, suddenly our float would appear—looking nothing like it had when we had stopped working December 30. Most people only saw the luscious lilies, blooming roses, and other flowers. Our eyes saw something different, however: every swipe of seeds, and every piece of bark. By the time the float appeared on television, our eyes were trained to look for details.

Something similar seems to be happening within Matthew's climatic parable today. Jesus was facing his last days. Having shared messages about his return throughout chapter 24, Jesus' teaching turned to pressing matters of persevering throughout difficult moments. His parables remind the disciples that details matter. He called them to pay attention by seeing things others might miss. In one example, he said that the kingdom of heaven would be like bridesmaids awaiting the arrival of a long-delayed groom. All of them became drowsy and fell asleep, but were awakened when the cry went out, "Look! Here is the bride groom." While all had become sleepy, the wise bridesmaids had planned ahead and made sure their lamps were trimmed and ready. The ones who were not paying attention were given the rather ridiculous advice to go out to the marketplace after midnight to buy more oil!

Next he told them that the kingdom would be like a businessman who entrusted his property to his slaves prior to leaving on a long journey. Each one of the slaves was given an enormous amount of money and told to manage it while the man was gone. Most of the slaves made sure their master's money was invested for a profitable return. Yet one saw things differently. He remained in fear of his master and decided to protect the money against all risk. That one buried his master's money — and while he returned the principal safe and sound, made no profit.

Once again, said Jesus, understanding the kingdom was a matter of seeing things differently. While the last servant protected his master's investment, he failed to see the opportunities the others imagined. From a kingdom perspective, seeing is truly believing.

Things changed a bit in this last parable. All of a sudden, Jesus was no longer a humble rabbi dependent on others. Instead, he returned "in his glory," and became seated on a throne of power. He gathered the nations before him as a shepherd gathers sheep and goats. He placed the sheep at his right hand, and the goats at his left.

Jesus rewarded those gathered at his right hand for their faithfulness. They were the ones who had fed Jesus when he was hungry, and who gave him something to drink when he was thirsty. They were the ones who had clothed him and welcomed him, and cared for him when he was sick or in prison. They were the ones who were invited to enter the glory of the kingdom.

On the other hand, the goats had not fared so well. They failed to feed Jesus, and did not welcome him. They did not clothe him or offer him something to drink. They did not visit him in prison or extend care to him when he was sick. They were sent, Matthew said, "into eternal punishment."

Right away we're presented with difficulties. Neither of the group claims they ever saw Jesus sick or in prison. None of them ever saw him hungry, or naked, or lonely. How was it that they saw him? How was it that others missed him?

Secondly, the parable runs the risk of arguing in favor of works righteousness. Instead of receiving the kingdom by grace, it seems as if only those who do the work can earn the prize. Such theology is a bit hard to swallow, perhaps especially at the tail end of indulgent holiday celebrations.

If that was the end of the parable, notes Tom Long, then we'd be left with nothing more than a conventional morality tale. Those who do good are rewarded, and those who fail to do what's expected are punished.[30]

Yet Jesus' words to us on this first day of the year are different. Neither group had seen Jesus. Both were simply going about their everyday activities. Both groups were incredulous: "We didn't see you there! How was it that we helped you, or how was it that we ignored you?"

The response, it seems to me, is a bit like the instructions we received while toiling away on those massive floats. Sitting high on the scaffolds, pushing seeds into sticky, goopy glue, we could never see what only the designers had imagined. Our work at times felt grueling and meaningless. "What's the point?" a few of us said. Indeed, we could probably imagine a few of the goats were thinking something similar: why bother noticing that person on the corner, especially when so many are hungry. Why bother taking the time to pay attention

30 Thomas G. Long, Matthew, ed. Patrick D. Miller and David L. Bartlett, Westminster Bible Companion (Louisville, KY: Westminster John Knox Press, 1997), 284.

to a child in distress, especially when there is so much other work we need to do? Why bother visiting that one family who drives us nuts?

Well, the answer to that question, according to Jesus, is a matter of perspective. "As you did it to one of the least of these are members of my family, you did it to me."

On this first day of a New Year, may these words of Jesus' final teaching challenge us. May they awaken us to seeing the holy masked behind ordinary faces of children, the elderly, or those in prison. May we be reminded to train our eyes the way Jesus has taught us.

A few years ago, I heard that a young person from our church had been arrested. I had known him for years, and frankly had feared that this day might come. His life was a complicated mix of mental illness and addiction. He had made poor choices throughout his life. For many years, he was able to skirt through those choices without many consequences. This time, however, was much different.

I decided to stop by the county jail to see him. I was not prepared for what I encountered. The young man who had once obsessed over his hair and clothes looked much different. His hair was matted and long, his beard unkempt. His orange jail clothes were hardly the sort of designer threads he enjoyed.

But it wasn't me who was the most surprised. At first, he didn't seem to recognize me. And then he wondered why I was there: was his family okay? Had something bad happened? "Nothing is wrong," I said, "I just wanted to let you know someone was thinking about you." It wouldn't be enough to erase the consequences of his actions, I thought, but it might be enough for him to know the surpassing grace of God.

It can be hard to train our eyes to see where God appears. And sometimes we won't get it right. Yet the possibility and hope of our faith is that as we lean into the teaching of Christ, we will begin to train our eyes to see things differently. And often, it appears, that will be in the surprised looks of the least of Jesus' family.

I imagine Jesus' instructions to be a bit like our experience working on the Rose Parade Floats. You do not always see the impact of your efforts. Our eyes are not trained to imagine the details that a float decorator imagines. That's why we were only paid a few cents an hour. The decorators, however, saw things differently.

Amen.

The Promise Of New Joy

In the beginning was the Word, and the Word was with God, and the Word was God. He was in the beginning with God. All things came into being through him, and without him not one thing came into being. What has come into being in him was life, and the life was the light of all people. The light shines in the darkness, and the darkness did not overcome it. (vv. 1-5)

Our neighbors were out taking down their lights and hauling their dried up Christmas trees to the curb. Most of the boxes had been picked up from the living room by now, and a few items had been exchanged. Our kids will get a few more days to sleep in, perhaps, but pretty soon it will be time to get back to reality. It's time to pack up Christmas until next year.

Statistics suggest that most Americans remain optimistic about the new year, which is somehow surprising when you realize that many of the big problems we faced in the previous year have yet to be settled. In 2022, researchers at the website YouGovAmerica noted about 86% of Americans believed that 2022 would likely be better than 2021, a sign that we continue to yearn for something fresh. I imagine such surveys remain consistent year after year.

Optimism inspires millions of people to make New Year's Resolutions in hopes of renewing those fleeting feelings of freshness. We fuel up on the power of positive thoughts as expressed by the French psychologist Emile Coue, who introduced the "autosuggestion" method made famous by repeating the inspirational mantra, "Every day, in every way, I'm getting better and better."

I once heard a story that illustrated that repeating that mantra can be dangerous. My father told me the story about a sales rep who was a miserable failure. The boss sent this rep to a seminar on positive sales strategies which included a workshop on using positive self-talk as a motivator for success. The problem was the man had a terrible memory and could never remember the mantra. He decided to tie a knot on a piece of string each time he repeated the words so he would not lose track. But that didn't work out so well, and soon the man fell far behind in sales and was called into his bosses' office. What was going wrong? The man told his boss he had no idea. Each morning, he said, he would get up and grab the string to start repeating the autosuggestion. "I get up in the morning," he told his boss, "And I pick up my string and then I recite, 'Every day, in every way, I am (knot) getting better; every day in every way, I am (knot) getting better."

An optimistic outlook is essential to our well-being, and positive self-talk is certainly part of that. Our faith, however, leads us to see that the fresh joy God offers goes well beyond positive self-talk.

John's prologue pushed us to see that the ultimate hope of our lives is grounded in wisdom that exceeds mere human optimism. John challenged us, in the words of author Joyce Rupp, to consider the New Year as God's gift of freshness that renews and nourishes our relationship with God. Freshness offers the opportunity to see hope growing out of the chaos and clutter of our old failures, struggles, and grief. John and Jeremiah upheld a vision of God's entrance and activity in our lives that is bold and invites us to live with renewed confidence. This freshness invites us to dare. It calls us to daringly imagine a year that is as fresh as clean sheets, as abundant and joyful as a new box of crayons, as crisp as the pages of a new book.

John's majestic prologue commanded our attention, calling us to imagine an abundant hope filled with new possibilities. It is a hymn of praise, an opening overture to the whole of the gospel. The verses echo the story of creation, working together to alert us to the promise of the incarnation. All of it centers on the promise that "the light shines in the darkness and the darkness did not overcome it."

One time during Christmas Eve worship, our son-in-law took a picture of the candlelight communion service. His wife, our daughter, shot him a look and said, "What are you doing?" But the photograph was amazing: his candle, sharp in focus, shining in the darkened sanctuary against a backdrop of less focused flickering candlelight.

There is the source of our new joy.

Do yourself a favor this afternoon. Pull out your family Bible and toss a log on the fireplace. Slowly read these words from John, chapter one. Let each word rest on your tongue for a moment and see if you can begin to hear the joy God is offering. Begin to imagine the new ways God is coming to us in the concrete realities of daily life.

Each new year, we are challenged with the task of allowing the light of God to burn bright. This was the joy I saw in the face of member of our church who died several years ago. John would show up on Saturdays to make sure the rows of the sanctuary were straightened and tend to several housekeeping chores. After making certain there were pens in the friendship pads and that the chancel table candles were filled with oil, John would poke his head into my office. He'd smile and say, "Well, the light of the Lord will burn bright tomorrow!"

I miss that man with my heart, but his words remain with me. As dark as it sometimes seems, the light of God's love shines brighter. I believe we discovered that reality during the depths of the pandemic. I believe we continue to experience that each day, even on those days when it seems as if everything is broken around us. We live with our legs planted in the broken, chaotic messiness of our world while our arms reach toward the promise of God's love. We have learned that the church is called to be those people who lean forward, who walk in the light.

We have learned that the light of the Lord will burn brighter tomorrow.

It is a documented phenomenon that death rates increase after the holidays — just ask a funeral director, healthcare worker, or pastor. I have two funerals scheduled for this week, and one more for the week to come. That is the reality of our lives. But the other reality is the God whose light continues to shine in the at darkness. It is easy, wrote Desmond Tutu, to be so "caught up in the clamor of the tragedy that fills the headlines" that we "forget about the majesty that is present all around us."[31]

Do we dare imagine what it might be like to live with a hope that is more than the power of positive thinking, more than an optimistic outlook?

Joyce Rupp, the writer I just mentioned, looked out her window one cold New Year's morning. What had once been a barren landscape was filled with the flourish of fresh snow. It created an amazing winter wonderland — sun streaking across the snow, tress outlined by the accumulating flakes, the world transformed. She wrote that she recalled a line from the poet Gerard Manley Hopkins, 'There lies the dearest freshness deep down things."

That is what God offers to us today: freshness, abundant possibility, a promise of new beginnings.

That "dearest freshness" is a sign of what God is about to do. We spend some time looking back at the year past, recalling the struggles, the losses, the hurts. It is the freshness of John's description of the incarnation, which, as one preacher has said, must be looked at by way of the losses and struggles we have endured:

What does the incarnation mean when over 800,000 bodies, at least in the United States, are no longer on this earth? Where and how is the church standing behind and up for bodies that are being beaten and broken? Demeaned and disregarded?

---

31 Tutu, *"God Has a Dream: A vision of hope for our time."* (Image Books, 2005).

Overlooked and oppressed? That are depressed and worn out? That are differently abled and aged? What does the incarnation really mean past December 25?[32]

What does it mean? It means the message of Jeremiah and the witness of John offer us a hope that goes far beyond feelings of optimism toward the hope of God's renewing and transforming presence.

It means we are offered the chance to keep the light of God burning.

One could never accuse Jeremiah of being a sunny side up sort of guy. He was not the sort of easy-going, happy-go-lucky sort of person you'd invite to a dinner party. He was, honestly, quintessential doom and gloom, end-is-near-repent or you'll be damned sort of prophet. Cheery words were not part of his every day vocabulary.

But in the chapters that we read this week, Jeremiah turned away from gloom. He embraced a particular sort of hope -not the sort of "things will get better, by and by," optimism, but a deep hope grounded in the promise of God who assures us: "I will turn their mourning into joy." These verses from Jeremiah point to the character of a God who remains in relationship with Israel, and who promises Israel that they will be renewed. The exile was not to be the end for God's people.

That is our good news: God gathers us together so that we may know the comfort of fresh joy. It is a gift to all who feel abandoned.

This is not only good news, but it is the heart of the message that we as God's people should be sharing with others. We live in a time when so many are running on fumes. So many are exhausted and beat up. We are anxious, worried. As we meet today, I know a church that is so weary, so exhausted, so anxious that they cannot imagine a future with their current pastor — and they will be voting quite soon to dismiss her. They have stopped seeing the freshness God offers.

32 https://www.workingpreacher.org/dear-working-preacher/light-shines-on-a-weary-world

Yet the light of the Lord still shines, and it will shine brighter tomorrow.

Amen.

Shall We Try Something Different?

My friend and writing colleague Katy Stenta said that her children have always called Epiphany the "Sneaky Kings Day." She explains that this passage is filled with "sneaky kings." The magi, who probably were not real kings, were found sneaking into Judea on a search for a newborn king. Talk about being sneaky! Usually kings use the front door, but Jesus had this way of just sneaking into the world. Meanwhile, after the magi visited Herod, the actual king of Israel, he began a secret mission to find out just who this newborn king really was, and where he might be holed up. There's a lot of sneaking around on Epiphany!

Epiphany is a big day throughout much of the world. In Latin American countries, it rivals Christmas for presents and family gatherings. "Dia de los Reyes Magos" is a day when magi leave presents for children in boxes they have filled with straw for the magi's camels. In the Netherlands, children dress as kings and queens and visit their neighbors' homes, sharing songs and receiving coins and sweets. In Ethiopia, Christians celebrate Epiphany as "Timcat" some two weeks after Christmas. They celebrate Jesus' baptism, and recall legends that suggest the magi delivered the Arc of the Covenant to Ethiopia upon their arrival.

Of course, since Epiphany is rarely on a Sunday, American Protestants have drifted away from Epiphany celebrations, seeing it as another day.

But what if we tried something different this year? Imagine the magi, turning the corner in Bethlehem. Guided by the star, they walk into this one stoplight village in search of the child whom they believe had been born king of the Jews. Their journey had taken them to a new destination. They had left their comfort zones behind and opened themselves to the possibility that God might be doing something new. So, my question to you is this: what are we going to do differently in this new year?

Epiphany — the manifestation of Christ — is the realization that the child in the manger is the living God who will lead us toward life abundant. We are invited to draw close to the abundance God provides for us. We are offered a chance to be surprised as we behold the miracle of what has happened. It is indeed a call to explore the new possibilities of faith through the eyes of those secretive sages, the mysterious magi whose adoration of Christ invites us to see the holiness of God incarnate.

Sometimes, the arrival of the wisemen in church Christmas pageants offers a bit of comic relief. We're offered an opportunity to giggle a bit at the kids adorned with Burger King® crowns and clad in their father's bathrobes. Snickering beneath their fake beards, they look more like the Three Stooges than the Three Wisemen, but what are you going to do?

Making their way toward the Child, they sometimes belch, trip, and giggle at themselves, and we do as well. How absurd! The kid who can't sit still in church suddenly becomes the one leading us to worship the newborn Christ. But here they come, and their arrival reminds us that God is still acting in surprising ways.

I think Matthew would nod his head in agreement at these slightly off-key representations of the magi. He has told us that Jesus shall be "Emmanuel," or "God with us," and now a tale of legendary proportions begins to be woven. He was, after all, the only one of the gospel writers to tell us this story, and I believe he may have told it with a slight twinkle in his eye. Imagine Matthew regaling the church with the angel's pronouncement to Joseph. He held his audience on the edges of their seats recounting God's promise to Joseph.

A second later, the scene shifted. Matthew cuts to the royal palace. "Imagine this," he told us, "out of nowhere appear up a band of starry-eyed dreamers who show up in the capital city asking a somewhat paranoid king where they might find the newborn challenger to his throne."

The magi frightened Herod — he was unaccustomed to foreigners inviting him to see things in new ways. "What is this?" he thought. "A new conspiracy? Some sort of rogue actor, or a deep-state attack on my power?" The news rattled him, and when the king was worried, the entire city was worried as well.

I was surprised to find out that the magi just happened to be in town this morning as part of their holiday tour. They've accepted my invitation to come and join us today, and I believe you'll be encouraged by what they have come to tell us. Without further ado, allow me to present to you, **The Three Magi!**

PASTOR	(As the musician plays "We Three Kings," the magi enter. Adults with good reading voices will make the best choices for these parts. This requires minimal preparation and costuming.) Siblings in Christ, it is indeed my honor to introduce to you these three mysterious visitors from the East. They've come here directly from their appearance in Judea, and they seem to have presents for us!
MUSICIAN	Opening lines of "We Three Kings of Orient Are."
PASTOR:	We welcome you, magi! Magi Number One, will you please introduce yourself….

CASPAR ("Magi #1)	(**Enters the sanctuary with a cart of donuts and pastries**). Greetings, friends! My name is Caspar, and I come from a far away and exotic place.
CHRIS:	And where is that, Caspar?
CASPAR:	Uh, El Paso. But I am delighted to join you for your Epiphany celebration. I have travelled long and far to be with you, and I bring you gifts that are sweet and delicious. (**Motioning to the pastor**) Do you know why I am sharing the gifts of donuts and pastries with you?
PASTOR:	I don't know…are you a baking magi?
CASPAR:	No, I am bringing you gifts of friendship and hospitality. Afterall, they do call me "Caspar The Friendly Magi!" I bring you these gifts as a reminder of the way God calls your congregation to the ministry of hospitality. Please enjoy them! But remember that that as God has welcomed each of us, so we are called to welcome those whom God sends our way. The gift of hospitality is a precious gift that demonstrates God's welcome and love for all.

PASTOR:	Thank you, Caspar, and please, everyone feel free to enjoy our donuts and pastries in honor of *"Dias de los Tres Reyes Magos,"* the traditional Latino celebration of the day of Epiphany. *(Other servers can help pass treats to the worshippers.)* As you enjoy the refreshments, let me introduce Magi Number Two. Melchoir, are you here? Has anyone seen Melchoir?
MELCHOIR:	(Melchoir enters singing a hymn like "We Three Kings," or some other easy hymn like "Amazing Grace." He is carrying a bag full of paper stars.) Hello, greetings and salutations, dear friends! It is I, "Mel Choir" [**say it like "Choir"**), the singing magi!
PASTOR:	A *singing* magi? I don't seem to recall that from the Bible.
MELCHOIR:	Well, some editor cut out that part. But here I am, "Mel" Choir: I sing, I dance, I tell jokes…not bad for a kid from Brooklyn, right?
PASTOR:	Brooklyn? I thought you were from Persia.

MELCHOIR: Persia? Where did ya' get that? The books say we're from the East. Me, personally, I'm from Brooklyn, you know, just a wise guy from the East! And just like Caspar, I bring a gift for you. I bring a treasury of hearts that will help you recall all the things you treasure about your church. Please take a moment now to form groups of three persons with the people near you. Share with each other what you treasure most about your church. Write down what you treasure on the hearts so that we can share these treasures with everyone later.

Please share with your neighbors now. As I leave, allow me to offer you one more little song: (*sung to the tune "We Three Kings"*) "I'm a king and I also sing. I tell jokes and make you smile. Oh, oh! Singing magi are such fun! Bringing treasures for all to see! Laughing, smiling, all enjoying God's good gifts today!"

PASTOR: Why, thank you, Mel! Please take a
                 moment to discuss, "What about our
                 church do I treasure most?" Please
                 write down your answers on the heart-
                 shaped paper. (*Give everyone a couple
                 of minutes, and then introduce Magi
                 #3*) Finally, friends, allow me to intro-
                 duce our final friend from the East...
                 Balthasar, aka "Magi #3," would you
                 please come forward?

BALTHASAR   Whoa, pastor, That's *Ms. Balthasar* to
                 you! These guys would never have got-
                 ten to Bethlehem if it wasn't for me!

PASTOR: This really is a new day! I never knew
                 one of the magi was a woman.

BALTHASAR	You think those guys would have ever asked for directions? My name is Balthasar, and my pronouns are indeed "She/her," and "Yes, ma'am!" Pastor, I am the scholar of the group. When the star of Bethlehem rose in the sky, I knew at once something important had happened. I consulted my charts and opened my heart to following the star. It led us to find Jesus, whom we have worshipped. I also bring you a special gift. It is the gift of vision and hope! Please take a few moments to write down your greatest hopes and prayers for your church on these paper stars. Allow them to become your prayers for this New Year! Let us all be guided by these stars in the new year!
PASTOR:	We thank you, wise friends, for coming to visit us today. As you are finished with your "hearts and stars," please pass them to the center and the ushers will collect them so we can post them next week.

Sermon concludes...

While Matthew does not tell us how many magi there were, nor did he let us know if they they rode camels, donkeys, or bicycles. But those details do not matter nearly as much as the reminder that they were guided by a vision that took them in a new direction. Then, when they reached their goal, Matthew reminds us that what they found changed their lives. "They left for their own country by another road."

Whoever they were or were not, it is clear that Matthew wants us to know that they were summoned to Christ by the brilliance of light. They were strangers, Gentiles, outsiders who had no understanding of the ways of the God of Israel. They were even a threat to the government. Herod would have been viewed as dangerous interlopers who should be excluded from Israel's worship and life.

But they were among the first to worship Christ. They were the first to see that the true King of Israel is not robed with power, but is instead a helpless infant, a child who would grow up to be wounded for his people. They were the ones who helped Matthew's church ask a critical question, "What is our next faithful step?"

Amen.

Immersed In Righteousness

"Then Jesus came from Galilee to John at the Jordan, to be baptized him..." (Matthew 3:13)

Standing with his toes in the water, Jesus looks at John as if to say, "Let's get busy with the mission God is giving us."

Once more, John's booming voice called us to the wilderness. There we saw his eyes widen at the sight of his cousin standing in the long and growing line. The line snaked up and around the banks of the Jordan, moving steadily toward the river. Compelled by the urgency of his message of repentance, throngs made their way to be baptized. He had warned them that the one who was coming will bring a baptism of fire and the Spirit — and now he's arrived.

Suddenly, John was faced with a surprising dilemma: why should Jesus be baptized? He realized that Jesus was going to offer something that surpassed anything John could administer. Moreover, why on earth would one without sin need a baptism for the repentance for sin? None of this makes much sense.

Within these four verses, Matthew offered a compact scene that raised the theological thesis of his unfolding gospel story. Jesus came to fulfill all righteousness — not only the forgiveness of individual sins, but also the redemption of all creation. Jesus stood in solidarity with those yearning for forgiveness, but he also came to fulfill a broader, more expansive righteousness.

Clearly, this would be no ordinary baptism.

But when are baptisms ever ordinary? Clearly it was no ordinary baptism when fourteen South Africans drowned during a river baptism a few years ago.[33] Likewise, when it was reported that a Phoenix priest had been using the "wrong words" during a baptism, a scandal broke out through the diocese.[34] Clearly, there are few baptisms we could call ordinary.

Pastors, of course, are no strangers to the dilemmas surrounding baptism. Frantic grandparents call late on a Saturday night wondering if the pastor could "do the baby" tomorrow morning before their kids fly home. Another family asked if the baptism could happen on a Wednesday night in their living room. Others get irritated when they ask the newly ordained pastor, a woman, if she would mind if they asked the ancient pastor emeritus, a man, to baptize their nephew. "You'll just ruin the whole experience," they snapped. The sacrament quickly becomes reduced to a commodity designed to meet individual needs.

While the story of Jesus' baptism is not a template for our own, his willingness to be immersed in the grimy waters of humanity was a reminder that baptism is more than an individual moment of personal spiritual clarity. It's our initiation into the household of God.

It is an invitation to be immersed in righteousness.

If ordinary baptisms cause headaches, then it's no surprise that Jesus waiting among the crowds was a sign of the higher righteousness that Matthew will highlight throughout the gospel. It's a clear indication that his ministry, his life, and all that he will proclaim will be deeply connected to community. He stood in solidarity with saints and sinners. The waters of this baptism rippled outward in broad arcs.

---

33 See https://www.yahoo.com/news/river-baptism-ceremony-ends-tragedy-190947510.html?guccounter=1

34 See: https://www.washingtonpost.com/nation/2022/02/15/catholic-priest-wrong-word-baptisms-invalid/

It's a reminder, said Thomas Long, that Jesus' baptism is "a symbol of his total involvement in the human condition."[35] But this may be a sticking point for those who prefer religion and faith to be a buffet line of personal choices. Those who have worshiped at the high altar of rugged individualism will be challenged by Jesus' call to community.

We saw this in the early days of the pandemic. Robin Nelson noted how the pandemic both tore apart our natural inclinations to remain gathered in groups while also exposing the weaknesses of hyper-individualism. She noted that communities which were invested in "social safety nets" such as paid sick leave, vaccine education, were more adept at handling the pandemic and lowering loss of life.

Meanwhile, said Nelson, many communities within the United States saw a more inconsistent response that bore the hallmark signs of cultural myths such as individualism and dehumanization of other persons. "As a result, even though we now know how the virus spreads and causes disease and we have effective vaccines against it, the death toll from Covid is higher in the US than anywhere else."

Jesus' baptism remains a sign of God's standing in our midst. Jesus shows up, knee deep in a large, messy, interconnected grace-filled pool of community. It's just how God knits together community.

A few years ago, a historic blizzard impacted millions along the northeast portions of the United States. In the middle of that snowstorm, Jay Withey of Kenmore, New York, found himself stuck in snow covered roads and dangerous temperatures. After knocking on more than a dozen doors pleading for sanctuary, Withey resigned himself to spending the night inside his truck. Along with his traveling companion and a woman they found stranded, the three hunkered down inside the vehicle while outside temps plummeted. By morning, Withey knew they needed to find warmth, water, and food.

---

35 Thomas Long, *Matthew*, p. 33.

"I look on a map on my phone, and I see there's a school nearby," Withey, said in an interview with *The Washington Post*[36]. He told the woman: "'I'm breaking into that school. I know there's heat in there, I know there's a bathroom, and I bet there is food.'"

Withey's decision to create this impromptu family may have saved dozens of lives. After breaking into the school, he returned to the streets searching for others who were lost. "My mission was just to keep going out and grabbing as many people as I can and to just keep going," Withey said. "I just kept walking, and I walked until I cried and I couldn't walk any further. I was just beat."

Inside the school, he found blankets and made Christmas dinner from school pizza. The group stayed about 24 hours until it was safe to leave. Before he left, Withey penned a quick note apologizing for breaking into the building — but also borrowed the school's snowblower so he could clear a path for the group. Bonded by tragedy, the group pledged to meet again for a party — sometime the next summer.

Matthew's account of Jesus's baptism drips with the details of a God who stands with us, who shows up, and who finds ways for us to dwell safely. Matthew set the scene by introducing John and his milieu. "In those days," Matthew began, tipping the hat to the *kairos* of the moment. Something important was about to happen, and Matthew's audience was summoned to full attention. The sense of anticipation continued to build with John's introduction and character description. There was a deepening sense of the moment's prophetic impact.

Unique to Matthew was the conversation between Jesus and John. Immediately John recognized Jesus. A pit grew inside John's stomach, and he knew it was more than just the locusts and honey he had for lunch. But Jesus intercepted his move to prevent him from being baptized, reminding John that "for it is proper for us in this way to fulfill all righteousness."

36 See https://www.washingtonpost.com/lifestyle/2022/12/31/buffalo-blizzard-jay-withey-rescue-school/

It was a stunning moment that raised all sorts of theological questions. If John's baptism was for repentance, then why was Jesus repenting? Moreover, what exactly did he mean about fulfilling "all righteousness?"

Matthew was showing his theological hand. Righteousness, a common theme to which he would return, was the centerpiece of Jesus' first words in the gospel. Fulfilling righteousness, scholars note, seemed to explicitly link Jesus to Old Testament prophesies describing God's desire to restore the world. Stanley Saunders underscored Matthew's intentions.[37] "Whereas modern audiences may think of righteousness primarily in terms of individual moral conduct, in Matthew, righteousness is focused on restoration and relationships made whole."

Thirdly, Matthew changed Mark and Luke's wording of God's affirmation of Jesus' identity. In the other gospels, God declared "You are my beloved Son," where Matthew offered, "This is my beloved Son." These words, repeated on the Mountain of Transfiguration, echoed Psalm 27, and were the heavenly affirmation of Jesus' authority. But that authority, it seemed, was also connected to his humbling of himself to John's baptism.

Standing with his toes in the river, Jesus seemed to be saying to John, "Let's get on with this work of building community."

Here is our change to rehydrate our awareness of baptism. With Martin Luther, we may raise our hands over our heads and repeat, "I too have been baptized" as reminders of the grace that surrounds us. Even if we were baptized sixty, seventy, or more years ago, John offered the chance for us to renew our understanding of what it means to be immersed in righteousness.

Thomas Long noted that there exists in Matthew 3 a rudimentary template for understanding the rites of Christian baptism. There are clear Trinitarian implications, allusions to the Old Testament, and a linking to Jesus' pathway of ministry.

37 Stanley Saunders, *Connections Commentary*, Year A, Volume 1, p. 174.

Jesus arose out of the water commissioned to be God's agent in the world, building a community of discipleship and faith.

Jesus' baptism, set against the rugged backdrop of wilderness, acknowledged his role in standing with both the religious elites who had come seeking John's baptism, as well as scores of brokenhearted, marginalized, fractured men and women. No surprise then that God would acknowledge and affirm Jesus as the beloved Son — for in Christ, God was at work repairing and renewing the world.

One Monday, I got a short text from a man who had received baptism the day before. He told me he was traveling for business, something that generally created intense waves of anxiety for him. That day, however, as he settled into the airplane, a new thought struck him. "I'm baptized," he remembered. "I matter to God and am part of a community that cares for me. For the first time in my life, I know I've found my community."

God is standing with us, immersed in our lives. This is the truth which reveals the hope of the gospel to us and allows us to discover the love God intends for us. Truly, it is proper for Jesus to be baptized in this way to fulfill all righteousness.

Amen.

What Are You Looking For?

The next day John saw Jesus coming toward him and said, "Look, the Lamb of God, who takes away the sin of the world! (v. 29)

Years ago, when our family was on vacation in Chicago, we ducked into a subway station to make our way back to the underground parking lot where we had left the car. We were immediately presented with two tunnels to the trains, neither of which was well marked. All of a sudden, a short, squatty man who looked as if he were homeless came up to me and said, "You look so (bleeping) lost." I backed up and then he flashed a badge. He was an undercover police officer, and to the delight of our kids was in the middle of arresting someone. But he kept giving me directions. "Where are you going?" and then pointed to the right tunnel.

Where are you going? What are you looking for? Not only were these the first words out of Jesus' mouth, they are also the sort of basic existential questions that guides us throughout our lives.

There was a time — and it feels like a long, long time ago — when exploring the answer to that question involved a long, slow search through the card catalog at the library. Thanks to Google®, we have sped up that search a bit, but it is still a fundamental question. What are you searching for? What makes life beautiful and wonderful? My wife told me that in all of her years in hospice ministry she never heard someone say "I wish I had a bigger bank balance," or "I wish I had more things."

Yet these are the things that consume much of our time: buying and selling, acquiring and gathering, and letting go.

Jesus asked this question to two of John the Baptist's disciples who had heard John proclaim, "Here is the lamb of God!" Here was the one who was sent to bridge the gap between human beings and God. Here was the proof that God had come to dwell with us. John testified that here was the one who would break the yoke of sin, and who would bring us abundant life.

Here was the one with whom God called you to abide.

"Where are you staying?" they asked. It was a verb that could also mean "abiding." Time and time again, Jesus would call the disciples to abide — to remain together. It is by abiding together that they would find the ways to eternal life. Abiding, like sheep grazing in a pasture, brings us closer to the answers we are looking for when we wonder if we are lost, alone, frightened. "What are you looking for?" And Jesus said, "Come and see."

As all of us know, this new year has not been particularly smooth sailing for many of us around Woodlawn Chapel. We have faced two sets of problems: ones that can be solved by insurance, and ones that will require God's gift of healing. A long time ago, Carol Keating and I decided that any problem that could be fixed by car insurance was not truly a problem. This was particularly helpful for us to remember when we had teenage drivers. Or, more correctly, when we had a teenaged male driver. It's a bit of an over generalization, but there is something calming about saying to yourself, "It's just a piece of metal. It's just a broken pipe. It's just a lot of drywall." I called a carpet contractor this week to get an estimate on repairing the cove molding. He asked if we needed to replace the carpet. I said, "No, just miles and miles of molding."

But that is really an inconvenience more than it is a problem. And, even if we did not have insurance or if the insurance would not pay, it would still be more of an inconvenience than a real problem.

But the other problems prove more painful. Just as we were struggling with the impact of flood waters, we were also confronted by the deaths of two of our own friends. Grief is more than just a problem; it is a complex series of reactions and feelings. I looked at the candles on the communion table the other day. I noticed they needed more wax, and I started to say, "I better call Bob..." Or I was thinking about who might host a fellowship event in their home, and all I could think about were the events that Peggy Swing hosted, or the classes she helped organize, or the long list of books she was always reading. Grief — both for individuals and for a church — is hard, much more than a simple problem to be solved. It is a journey to be experienced. If we love someone, we will grieve them.

And if we grieve, we grieve not as people who have no hope, but as people who have known that God has come close to us in Jesus Christ. We grieve using the words of Psalm 40: "I waited patiently for the Lord; he inclined to me and heard my cry. He drew me up from the desolate pit, out of the miry bog, and set my feet upon a rock, making my steps secure. He put a new song in my mouth, a song of praise to our God. Many will see and fear and put their trust in the Lord." Grief is hard and uncomfortable, but it remains something we will all experience.

We grieve, wondering if there is an answer to our deepest questions. What are we looking for? What do we want? Michael Rinehart reminded us that in John, Jesus was always shifting the small talk toward deeper questions. A woman was talking about water, but Jesus talked about spiritual thirst. Nicodemus asked how one can be born a second time from their mother's womb, but Jesus shifted it to a conversation regarding spiritual birth. We grieve or feel lost, and Jesus shifts our focus to the possibility that we will never need to be lost again.

As I was thinking about our good friends Bob and Peggy who both died last week, I remembered that, along with their spouses, they were once newcomers to Woodlawn Chapel. They were once visitors who walked through those doors uncertain of what they would encounter, unsure if this would be a community of welcome, unsure if this would become a place where they would invest themselves. They came to us with experiences at other churches, some good, some not so good. Peggy was quick to say she was always up for an adventure, and my kids remember Bob as the older man who drove a Jeep Wrangler®. They came with their own questions, but they also came searching for something more. They laughed with us, cried with us, hugged us, and now they cheer us on as we continue our journeys. In their struggles and pain, joys and smiles, both taught us all a bit more about what it means to be disciples of Jesus Christ.

In my own grief, I am finding tremendous comfort in remembering that both of these saints died in the time right after Christmas. In this Epiphany season, we are called to hit the reset button. We are summoned to testify, like John, to what we have seen and heard.

John, with his voice filled with excitement and energy, called us to find what we are looking for most. All that he did was an act of witness that pointed to Jesus Christ — something most of us feel completely inadequate and ill-prepared. You remember the old joke: "What do you call religious people who knock on your door but have nothing to say? Presbyterians." Witnessing is not something which comes natural to us.

The question is more than an abstract philosophical debate. Jesus was inviting us to come and see, to experience the calling of God in our lives. What are you looking for? A religious experience? A spiritual moment of divine clarity? Are you looking for the answers to lifelong search for meaning? I am aware that some people see faith as nothing more than a distraction, or a set of guidelines for raising good children. But Jesus was not interested in handing over a plan for effective families. He was not concerned with giving us the answers to a happy life. He asked deeper, more probing questions: "What are you seeking?" and "What is your dream?"

Sixty years ago, a young minister stood on the steps of the Lincoln Memorial and said, "I have a dream." We often focus so much on Martin Luther King Jr's public witness that we forget his calling to that role was nurtured in the everyday work of being a pastor. Doctor King was a visionary, a peacemaker, an activist — but he was first a Christian. "My call to ministry," he once wrote, "was neither dramatic nor spectacular. It came neither by some miraculous vision nor by some blinding light experience on the road of life. Moreover, it did not come as a sudden realization. Rather, it was a response to an inner urge that gradually came upon me."[38]

It came as he abided in Christ, experiencing the tap of the shoulder of one who calls us to be focused on what really matters in life.

Amen.

---

38 https://kinginstitute.stanford.edu/king-papers/documents/my-call-ministry

What Is Shelter?

As Jesus was walking beside the Sea of Galilee, he saw two brothers, Simon called Peter and his brother Andrew. They were casting a net into the lake, for they were fishermen. (vv. 18-19)

Sometimes you can become so familiar with a story from scripture that you miss a little detail that can change the entire meaning. Something like that happened to me recently as I was re-reading Matthew's familiar story of Jesus calling the first disciples. The story is well known to us: Jesus, walking along the lakeshore, saw this big fisherman Peter, and his brother Andrew. They were working, making a living, and suddenly Jesus disrupted their business plan by calling out to them. "Follow me," he said, "And I will make you fish for people." We have heard that story, we have told that story, and we have passed it along from generation to generation.

And the typical lesson that preachers draw from that is that Jesus calls and we follow. The message to the church is clear: Jesus was calling us go to fishing. We're to sink our lines into the seas of our neighborhoods and reel in anything that bites, but the biggest prizes are the fish most likely to repopulate the church nursery. Sometimes preachers have been known to tweak the story a bit, using it as a reminder to sign up to teach Sunday school or make coffee, or other housekeeping tasks that keep the church running. "Remember," we tell someone, "Jesus said follow me and I will teach you how to make coffee for fifty people!"

But perhaps you have also experienced this. Sometimes, as you re-read something you have read hundreds of times before, a little detail will stick out. It's like an earring that got lost in the carpet. You've looked over the same area for hours when suddenly something glimmering catches your attention. I had that sort of experience recently when a friend pointed out to me a detail in this text that I had never before noticed.

It's there in verse thirteen at the beginning of today's reading. "He withdrew to Galilee. He left Nazareth and his home in Capernaum by the sea." Other translations say "he settled" in Galilee.

It's a little detail in Matthew 4 that almost escapes our attention. Chapter four of Matthew is packed with action and movement. It began with Jesus being tempted in wilderness, continued with the enlistment of the first disciples, mentioned numerous healings, and announced the start of Jesus' ministry. "Repent, for the kingdom of heaven has come near," Jesus told us. But all of this activity seems to center around this striking detail, unique to Matthew's gospel. "He left Nazareth," we are told, "and made his home in Capernaum by the sea" (4:13).

It sounds charming. Afterall, who doesn't want a place by the water?

But Jesus' relocation was not about setting up housekeeping in a seaside bungalow. He wasn't decorating with statues of gnomes in bathing suits or adding nautical flair to his cabana with cute sayings like "Life is a Beach." Matthew quietly inserted a theological detail that telegraphs an important aspect of Jesus' message. Capernaum isn't Jerusalem. It isn't the city of David. It's a working-class fishing village that would never be featured on a Cabin Masters or HGTV.

Jesus withdrew to Galilee, which is the same verb used when Joseph and Mary fled the wrath of Herod. He wasn't settling into life in a sleepy little fishing village. He was, rather, moving into dangerous territory. Galilee, geographically distant from the religious power center of Jerusalem, was nonetheless occupied and controlled by Rome's puppet Herod Antipas. It was a commercial center whose production of fish was tightly regulated and taxed by Rome — a peasant economy controlled by power hungry elites who would do anything to maintain their power.

For Jesus, "shelter" did not mean finding a nice place in the suburbs. Nor did it mean digging a bunker in the backyard. For him, shelter was in that part of town where we might make sure our windows were rolled up and our doors locked at all times. When Jesus settled down, he moved into hostile territory. This was the place where he called the first disciples: a working class neighborhood where poor fishermen barely managed to make a living wage. This was the place where Jesus sheltered. This was where Jesus made a home.

"Home," said poet Robert Frost "is the place where, when you have to go there, they have to take you in." In the past several years, home had also come to mean the place, when you have to go to school, you go online. Or home as the place where we earn our living. Home also became the place of quarantine and also a place of refuge: a safe place, to be sure, but also a place that can feel isolating and lonely.

Perhaps, as the psalmist said, the place where we find the shelter God can provide.

When the recent winter storms in California caused massive flooding, mudslides, and destruction, they proved disruptive not only for millions of homeowners but also for many thousands of homeless people. A reporter caught up with a 44-year-old woman who was mucking her way through a muddy field back to a makeshift compound where she lived. He asked her why she didn't go to a shelter. She hemmed and hawed a bit, talked about her dogs and how she would care for them. But then she said, simply, "Shelter? What is that?"

Psalm 27 offers a similar vision of faith. It is a psalm of trust and faith that has been hewn from the stones of conflict and struggle. The psalmist's question, "Of whom shall I be afraid?" may sound rhetorical, but I believe behind it is a whole host of fears. We could name them: fear of feeling lost, fear of failing, fear of aging, of getting sick. Of whom shall we be afraid? O, let me count the ways.

Yet the psalmist trusted that God is in the places where those fears live. The psalmist reached back into the memory of Israel to trust in the promises of God's steadfast love. That love seems to flow from his memory of being gathered into a community of worship. "One thing I asked of the Lord, that will I seek after: to live in the house of the Lord all the days of my life, to behold the beauty of the Lord and to inquire in his temple." So, it seems, while we may indeed be able to behold God's beauty and grace anywhere in this world, there is a deep promise of shelter conveyed in worship.

What is shelter? It is the promise of God revealed in gathering with God's people.

What is shelter? It is the promise of a God who gathers us into a community, drawing us away from the places where others seek to control and manipulate us. Jesus called the disciples away from meaningless lives of routine and struggle. Jesus, Emmanuel, dwells with those whose lives feel empty and lost.

Shelter is the refuge where God dwells, but it is also the mission Jesus calls us to pursue. This makes me think of six sentences that Presbyterians have used for hundreds of years as a guide to mission. They are not scripture, of course, but these "great ends" speak to the promises of faith. They read: The Great Ends of the Church are the proclamation of the gospel for the salvation of humankind; the shelter, nurture, and spiritual fellowship of the children of God; the maintenance of divine worship, the preservation of the truth, the promotion of social righteousness, and the exhibition of the kingdom of Heaven to the world."

Jesus dwells with us, and with those most at risk, and Jesus calls the church to go to those places, saying, "The kingdom of God has come near."

What is shelter? Perhaps it is the place where God's children learn they are accepted and loved. Shelter is the place where we can go fishing with God.

When I think about fishing stories, I almost always think about my buddy Carson. Carson died the other day. He was just eighteen years old, and died from complications of diabetes. He loved to fish, which is why his mom loaned me his fishing rod today. Carson was not an official member of our church, but Carson and his family have been important parts of our community for eighteen years. You might say Carson was one of the fish who have swum around us.

Carson lived a full life, though. He loved things that went fast and had a pile of speeding tickets to prove it. He was one of the hundreds of children who have come to our Mom's Day Out program. He was a loyal part of our Vacation Bible School all the way through high school. It was in these doors that Carson learned his identity that he was a beloved child of God.

As he grew up, Carson struggled with being a teenager with diabetes. He never quite said it, but you could tell that it was hard trying to keep up with friends while also managing his illness. Life was hard for him in other ways, but the one thing I loved about him was he would never fail to meet up with me for dinner or for conversation or even a simple text message. He knew this church to be a place of shelter.

Carson's father split from the family when he was little, leaving his mom with three kids. She worked hard, but being a single parent and having children with chronic illnesses is not easy. As he grew up, sometimes Carson and his mom would be at odds with each other. Sometimes he'd just get up and leave the house, telling her he was going out to fish. I think sometimes that was an excuse to get away from his mom, sometimes it was just a reason to take his old Jeep over muddy hills, either way, he went fishing to find a sheltering place.

I like to think the moments he spent in this church — helping with VBS, setting up science experiments for Mrs. Norvell, talking with me were also moments when he found shelter. Whether it was setting his line in the river or asking questions about life, Carson found his sheltering place.

Friends, this is what we as a church are called to do: to go and accept our identity that we are called to fish. To go and to know that God is with us, God is calling us, that we are to follow.

One night, I was working on a sermon about Jesus' calling of the disciples. I had just typed the words, "Follow me," when my phone rang with the news that one of our good friends from church had died.

When I returned from the hospital that night, I looked at the computer, unsure of how I'd approach the sermon. I could not find the words I wanted to say. But then I looked at what I had written hours earlier, and realized the sermon was finished: "Follow me."

In our times of grief — whether that is the loss of a dear friend, a family member, or any sort of loss that we may experience — what becomes essential is relearning what it means to find places of shelter. We learn what it means to trust as Jesus says to us, "Follow me."

Of course, we'll wonder. "I'm not sure," I've told God, especially in those times when friends have died. "I'm not sure, Lord, because it seems to me that trusting in this moment will require leaving behind everything that I have ever known." I mean, on a good day, I'm not always sure I can trust myself — how in the world can I learn to trust God? Is God to be trusted?" These are the essential questions we must ask ourselves before we can answer Jesus' invitation.

I'm not sure what made the disciples leave everything behind to follow Jesus; and I am equally not sure I would be able to do the same. It's an honest question: someone you do not know comes up to you and invites you to go someplace you have never been. It would be natural to ask ourselves, "Can he be trusted?"

There's an old prayer which I turn to from time to time. It was written by Theresa of Lisieux, a nineteenth-century French nun. It speaks of trusting in God's promise of shelter and hope:

Just for Today

Just for today, what does it matter, O Lord, if the future is dark? To pray now for tomorrow I am not able. Keep my heart only for today, grant me your light — just for today. Amen.

The Beatitudes — What Did He Say?

When Jesus saw the crowds, he went up the mountain; and after he sat down, his disciples came to him. Then he began to speak, and taught them, saying: "Blessed are the poor in spirit, for theirs is the kingdom of heaven...
Both the Beatitudes and Micah 6:1-8 offer a clear and succinct understanding of following God's will by acting justly, loving kindness, and walking humbly with God.

Jesus saw the crowds, climbed the mountain, and began preaching. He assumed the aura of Moses teaching the people of Israel, commanding attention, delivering the words of God.

His words echoed across the canyon, bouncing around. It felt a bit like a Super Bowl-sized extravaganza, a half-time show minus the fireworks and blasting of electronic music and amplified animation.

Jesus was preaching, speaking directly to the crowds who had been following him. His fame and reputation had been growing, and so had the hoards who were following him. He had been preaching the good news of the kingdom and offering healing throughout Galilee. He had made a name for himself, so much so that, in Matthew's words, "they brought to him all the sick, those who were afflicted with various diseases and pain, demoniacs, epileptics, and paralytics.

A large crowd, pulled from their ordinary routines, straining to hear what Jesus had to tell them.

But were they listening?

In an old, sacrilegious but extremely funny movie, the Monty Python comedy troupe portrayed this scene. Using their usual slapstick British humor, the troupe imagined what it might have been like for those who were late to the Sermon on the Mount. One ne'er-do-well disciple, Brian, found himself arguing with his mum, played by the great Terry Jones. "Speak up," Jones yelled toward Jesus. "Can't 'ear a thing he's sayin'!" As Brian tried to keep his mum quiet, someone else turns around and said, "I think he said 'Blessed are the cheesemakers.'"

The bit goes on and on: Blessed are who? What did he say? We laugh, but there's a bit of truth hiding in the comedy of that old movie. It points to a real dilemma for those who believe. Jesus climbed a mountain, sat down and spoke, but there was a big difference between hearing and understanding.

Blessed are *who*? What did *he* say? Say what? The scene evokes laughter while also pointing to a dilemma faced by people of faith. We struggle to articulate Jesus' words to our generation, but in the process mangle the syntax or confuse the meaning. Too often we fail to hear what Jesus has so clearly stated.

Our hearing problems become amplified. Jesus clearly articulated what it meant to seek the kingdom of God. It meant placing the values of God ahead of the concerns of the world. It meant adopting the words Micah proclaimed as our daily invocation of God's presence in our lives: to do justice, to love kindness, to walk humbly before our God.

Jesus said, "Blessed are the poor in spirit," not because he wanted to cheer up the lonely and scared, but to remind those who live on the edges of society that they were the object of God's greatest concern. He saw the destitute, the poorest of the poor, and recalled the words of Psalm 34:18, "the Lord saves those who are crushed in spirit."

He said, "Blessed are those who mourn," not because he called us to turn our frowns upside down, but because he reminded us that God understands the pain of those whose lives have been emptied by the power of death.

He said, "Blessed are the meek, the merciful, the pure in heart, the peacemakers," not because they make nice sound bites, but because these are the actual places where God is at work mending the broken hearts of the world.

Jesus was preaching from the mountain; but are we listening? Do we hear what he is saying?

Our world does its best to drown out Jesus' words about peace, making them sound irrelevant, or even foolish. Think of Jesus saying "blessed are the peacemakers," and recall that only a short time ago the "Bulletin of Atomic Scientists" took the extraordinary step of moving the minute hand of the figurative doomsday clock on the masthead of their publication twenty seconds closer to midnight. That is closer than it has ever been, even during the days of the Cold War. They warn us that the world is just a figurative 100 seconds away from global annihilation.

Perhaps you heard the uproar that happened recently when a small Methodist church in suburban Minneapolis took the unusual step of announcing it was going to close its doors for six months in order to be "reborn" as a different sort of church. Members of the Cottage Grove United Methodist church were angered when denominational leaders told them they were going to "rebrand" the church in an effort to attract younger members. An official encouraged older members to go to a different church — a not so subtle way of saying, "We're trying to do something different." News reports began circulating that the pastor and bishop were pushing older members to the curb. The actual intent of the denomination was more nuanced, but it was clear few people had heard what they were saying.

Jesus speaks to us today, speaking words of healing to the brokenhearted, the grieving, the outcasts. His word ricochets across the centuries. He speaks, but do we hear what he says?

On the one hand, the answer is yes. Both the Beatitudes and the passage from Micah are lush, familiar, and poetic. We know these words. They offer us comfort in a time of our own grief, and they speak to our highest hopes of what it means to be a Christian.

On the other hand, however, as Jesus speaks, the words also rub across us like sandpaper. They sound wonderful but are overwhelmingly impractical. They are foolish: blessed are the meek? When did that ever work out for somebody? They are impossible: blessed are the peacemakers? How can we live without a strong defense?

In our divided country, these words invite us to be transformed.

Listen to what the prophet Micah told us. Micah was pleading with God's people to recall the essence of God's love for them. He saw how their world had collapsed into a religion of empty rituals, a society of harsh oppression, and a faith built on winks and nods more than God's mercy.

Micah told them, "You know what you are to do. Listen to God: do justice, love with God's everlasting, steadfastness, walk in humility.

We can say these words. Practicing them is quite another thing.

We are now knee deep into a year of political debate. It will be a time of assessing the direction we believe our beloved country should take. Before you push the "post" button on Facebook, or before you enter into even the friendliest of discussions with coworkers, or stir the pot with family members whom you know disagree with you, ask yourself this question: Is what I am about to say, publish or post reflective of the transformation God offers?

Jesus is speaking. But the question remains: are we paying attention?

The word "lovingkindness," by the way, does not mean "being nice." Instead, it is the Hebrew word is "*hesed*," which always describes God's long-suffering patience and mercy. What God expects of us is to love with that sort of love. God yearns for that sort of steadfast mercy which wipes away the tears of the lonely and stands with the outcast.

It is all that simple, and all that hard.

My father's mother was a sweet, practical woman who was one of nine children. They lived in Virginia's Shenandoah valley and were raised on a small farm. Grandma soon realized that the world was bigger than that small town, so she and a couple of her sisters moved to Chicago. My father liked to tell the story of how she and her sister, his aunt, would go to the doctor in the depression for some sort of vaccination. Grandma's sister was very proud; she always got dressed to the nines, put on extra makeup, and wore her fancy jewelry. Grandma was more practical: she wore a simple dress, no makeup, and a simple coat. They both went to the doctor at the same time, but guess which one got a higher bill?

Grandma valued practicality and humility. When her father died, her family was beset by division and fighting as her siblings raced to the courthouse to probate his estate. They were divided: four on one side, five on the other, and soon they were not speaking. Lawsuits followed and all sorts of acrimonious words exchanged.

Meanwhile, Grandma kept talking. She made phone calls and paid visits. She brought canned goods and baked cookies. She arranged dinners and spoke kindly.

There are all sorts of reasons why it is impractical and foolish for the church to proclaim messages of peace. But it is still the right thing to do. It is what Jesus calls us to do, but I wonder if we are listening.

Amen.

The Last Of The Christmas Candles

Sometimes during the holidays, I will sit in a quiet place and allow the memories of years past to flow across my consciousness. There are times when I think about memories of years past when adrenaline flowed as mighty and fast as a mountain creek. I found myself thinking about those mornings when our children were young and they raced out of bed at breakneck speed only to crash into the one rule our family had on Christmas morning: no one goes downstairs until everyone is up.

Invariably worn out by Christmas Eve, I was rarely the first one out of bed. I will confess that I often played this to my advantage, and that our children routinely found this irritating. Actually, they still find it irritating even though most of them are no longer living at home! The more they became irritated, the slower I would move.

On some Christmas mornings, I would move even slower…purposefully rising from bed like a zombie, one limb at a time…slowly moving across the room as the kids were jumping up and down on our bed, clamoring through the upstairs hallway. I would rummage around pretending to being unable to find clothes while they sat wiggling on the top of the stairs. "Carol," I would say, "Does this shirt go with these pants? Have you seen my brown socks?" One year I ran into the bathroom and turned on the shower—only to hear one of our daughters say, "That's it! I'm going downstairs!"

Anticipating Christmas morning might be more exciting than actually tearing open the presents — or, as Winnie the

Pooh said, there was a moment before eating the honey that was actually better than the next moment, but he never knew what it was called.

But what remains when the anticipation is over?

Take a look at this box of candles from our Christmas Eve candlelight service. Some of them look a bit worse for the wear, don't you think? Some of these candles are bent, some of the holders show signs of carbon build up, some that are just plain old need to be thrown away. But, since we're a church, we'll find a way to keep reusing them well past their useful life!

This is what sometimes remains in our lives when the exhilarating moments are over. What remains are the less exhilarating, not-so-exotic, everyday rituals that connect the dots of our lives and in their own way add richness and texture to our lives. If the pandemic has left us with any lasting lessons of faith it is this: there is untold value in those sorts of everyday rituals. And it is those moments that we miss perhaps more than anything else: running into stores at the drop of a hat, dropping by to see friends, going to church on the Sunday after Christmas.

It is both the memories of Christmas mornings of unbounded energy and the everyday moments of life that are caught by Luke in this short snapshot of Jesus' life. The angels had returned to heaven, the shepherds had gone back to their flocks, Mary's pulse had returned to normal. Luke spilled out this story in exacting detail — Mary and Joseph headed to the temple in Jerusalem to perform the rituals required of them by the law.

There were two parts of these rituals: one was the rites of naming and circumcising Jesus, and the other the ritual of purification involving an offering. While these stories were recorded in a matter-of-fact manner, it is clear that there was a deeper message that Luke was conveying. In these vignettes about Simeon and Anna, Luke took what was ordinary and normal and transformed it into the church's Christmas morning experience of receiving the gift of the Christ child.

It was with the breathless excitement of Anna that the church received its hope, and it was with the holy anticipation of Simeon that people of faith were and are filled with the gift of God's peace — a gift that is perhaps especially important in times that are unusual, difficult, and even painful. The sense of anticipation remains. And it is even more important now.

It is more important than ever for people of faith to live in anticipation of all that God has promised. In an Advent-themed prayer, Walter Brueggemann put it this way: "Give us the grace and the impatience to wait for your coming to the bottom of our toes to the edges of our fingertips."[39]

In this confusing world of pain and bewildering circumstances, we find our deepest joys not in the tinsel and garland or even nostalgic memories of Christmas past, but in the promise that the hope we need comes to us in this child.

This is the prayer of the church this Christmas Sunday: infuse us with anticipation that dares to wait like Simeon and Anna, trusting in God's promised redemption. This is the prayer which became the hope that guided the steps of these two elderly saints of Israel, and it is our hope today.

It is a faith that keeps us singing — even when the church is apart, even when worship is not exactly the way we want it — even when the pastor has been forced to become an instant "expert" on video technology. (I put expert in quotation marks.)

Simeon and Anna were two of the least known characters in the Christmas story. They made cameo appearances only in Luke's gospel, but their stories were essential. Luke told us that Simeon had longed for the promise of Israel's comfort, and that throughout his life he had been guided by the Spirit. Simeon has lived with a nagging sense that God was about to do something new. His life has been spent in eager anticipation of the work Isaiah had promised:

> *Every valley shall be lifted up, and every mountain and hill be made low; the uneven ground shall become level, and the rough places a plain.*

39 Walter Brueggemann, *Awed to Heaven, Rooted to Earth*, p. 148.

Even in the most difficult, complex, and disappointing moments of his long life, Simeon refused to give up. God's comfort would come to him.

The same was true for Anna, an elderly widow, whom Luke euphemistically said "never left the temple." We know those sorts of dear people: the Annas who are faithfully in church, every Sunday, the old Simeons who bend down to coo at a young couple's baby, who speak to children, who form the essence of the interconnected, inter-generational church we love.

So, on that day when Mary and Joseph attended to the ritual laws of Israel, Simeon was there at the temple. Like an anxious toddler strapped into a car seat for a long ride, Simeon had grown weary of waiting. He and his family had spent hours playing rounds of "I spy with my little eye," always looking around the temple for signs of God's promise. He was looking on that day, unwilling to give up, when suddenly Mary and Joseph carried their baby into the temple.

I spy with my little eye....the Messiah!

His response has become an essential song of faith. Simeon's song, called the "Nunc Dimittis," is a benedictory, a blessing of one generation to the next: "Now let your servant go in peace according to your word, because my eyes have seen your salvation."

And even though Anna's eyes were clouded with cataracts, she also saw the child. She knew here was the fulfillment of all God had promised her. She knew that this child would bring about the promised redemption. Like a child who has just seen her most-hoped for Christmas present under the tree, Anna sang praise to God. Anna called us to sing — even if our voices crack just as bad as our knees, even if we are old, even if we believe we do not have anything left to sing.

Anna and Simeon sang. They shouted. They cried out, because their eyes have seen the salvation of God. Guided by the Spirit, they were in the right place at the right time.

One of the great scholars of American religious history is Albert Raboteau from Princeton University. In his research of American slave religion, Raboteau discovered the gospel of the enslaved church was shared in its songs. The meaning of faith is conveyed in the gospel song,

> *I will trust in the Lord. I will trust in the Lord. I will trust in the Lord till I die.*
> *I'm gonna stay on the battlefield, I'm gonna stay on the battlefield, I'm gonna stay on the battlefield, till I die.*

It was this conviction which allowed a people beaten, enslaved, and broken to bear witness to a hope that had been denied them for generations.

Friends, do you realize just what it might mean if the church — scattered as we are — might begin to sing of God's peace? The virus saps everything from us. Creation is polluted. Poverty is overwhelming. Yet the world waits for us to sing.

Simeon would have known that song. Anna knew it as well, and we should too. The church on Christmas morning sings of this hope.

Hope motivates us. Hope may seem absurd. Walter Brueggemann had taught us that it flies against everything the culture tells us. It dares to imagine new possibilities: lives deeply connected, love faithfully shared, grace extravagantly displayed.

Writing in the dark pessimism of the Cold War, Howard Thurman noted that "hope is the mood of Christmas; the raw materials are a newborn baby, a family, and work…hope is the growing edge…all around world are dying out, new world are being born…therefore I will light the candle of hope this Christmas that must burn all the year long."

On Christmas morning and the mornings afterward, let us run breathlessly downstairs in joyful anticipation, lighting the candle of hope. And it must burn all year long.

Amen.

Hiding In Darkness

Called to be salt and light, the church reveals the healing love and promises of God.

Light, as Jesus indicated, is meant to shine. It brings healing, empowers hope and scatters the clouds of lies. God's always-creating power brings light, and with it the end of deception.

Indeed, as the Washington Post's motto declared, "democracy dies in darkness." While not everything depends on light for life, it is essential for matters of truth telling and human survival. It's no wonder Jesus called the disciples to be lights shining in a darkened world.

But a shining light can be disruptive or disorienting. When light floods the darkness, we avert our eyes, struggling to let our pupils adjust to the change. Sometimes our inclination is to remain in the darkness — something Jesus no doubt understood in his warnings to the disciples.

When fans of basketball legend Kobe Bryant began processing his death, there were many who preferred to see only the rosy hues of the light of his celebrity. The complexities of his life were blunted by the tragedy surrounding his death as well as the deaths of his daughter and other passengers. Emotional tributes were offered by athletes, fans, celebrities, and more. Reporters rightly called him one of the greatest basketball players of all time.

Bryant's stature in culture loomed larger than his towering 6'6" frame. In retirement, his fame spanned the breadth "of the entire internet," including a multimedia empire, children's books, and an Oscar winning movie, *Dear Basketball*.

But the brilliance of his accomplishments could not hide the very credible accusations of sexual assault which Bryant faced. When these accusations were recalled following his death, reporters were condemned for their insensitivity. In an attempt to tell the truth, the media stepped on sensitive emotions.

The lesson is that we are always tempted to see just the good things in people's lives when they die. The ancients advised that we should never speak ill of the dead, which seems to be the rule enforced by most mourners attending North American funerals. Hang around a funeral home long enough, and you become convinced that only good people die. Whether out of courtesy or hesitancy to step out on the thin ice of grief, we generally demur from what one minister used to call "the full picture" of the deceased's life. As one man once said to me following a funeral of a rather bitter and recalcitrant church member, "Well, you certainly made that nasty old so and so sound pretty good."

It's a dilemma. One wants to be respectful and compassionate; but covering up the totality of a person's life does little to promote healing. A wise pastor proceeds cautiously, but faithfully. Experts say that the two most common forms of hagiography -- the practice of only speaking positively of the dead — are enshrinement or bedevilment. Enshrinement focuses only on celebrity's positive accomplishments. Bedevilment involves negating their humanity. Neither facilitates healing.

Meanwhile, the scriptures call us to live lives of integrity and honesty. Jesus calls us to be salt and light in the world. Salt is coarse and sharp. It heightens the senses, preserves food and stimulates thirst. Light creates new possibilities and offers hope. Jesus reminded the disciples that their presence in the world is to be both challenging and healing. He demanded that his followers surpass the considerable standards of piety established by the Pharisees — a high bar, indeed. Those called by Jesus are expected to act differently in their demonstrations of faithfulness. We are flavor that brings a new edge to God's creation, and the light which reflects the rays of God's gracious mercy.

Salt and light. This is the identity bestows upon the disciples. He made it plain that the work of faith is no private matter, no side deal with God. Instead, the life of faithfulness is to be displayed publicly. And he was quite clear: those whom he had gathered and blessed — this rather odd ball group of people — fisher folk and tax collectors, husbands and wives, homemakers, the sick, and disenfranchised — are the very ones through whom the realities of the kingdom will be manifest. He reminded these somewhat ordinary and powerless folks that they would be the ones who inherited the kingdom of heaven, and that they would be peacemakers, and even that they will be the ones who hungered and thirsted for righteousness.

And he revealed their identity, their trademark: they would be salt for the earth, and light for the world.

These were the indisputable marks of those whom God called. Jesus made it clear that even though the world may view them as powerless and meek, God had other plans. They have a role that is essential and critical: as flavorful and important as salt, and as essential to life as light. It is not the institutions of Israel which will be the signs of the kingdom. It is not even the Torah, or traditions of Moses. Rather, the essence of what it means to be the particles of God in this universe are found in these human bodies: salt and light.

Shane Claiborne is an interesting Christian writer who was a member of the generation following the Baby Boomers who are largely absent from the contemporary church — we call the folks born in his generation "Generation X," which is unfortunate, but it conveys the struggle that they feel being raised in the shadow of Baby Boomers. While in college, Claiborne and some friends became involved helping a group of homeless people who had moved into an abandoned church in North

Philadelphia and were being evicted. As radio host and author Krista Tippett says, "the irony was not lost on them."

It was at this point that Claiborne and his friends began asking hard questions: Had the church lost its zest, its purpose? They wondered if Jesus would recognize what was happening in the churches where they had been raised. He and his friends began asking, "Does anyone believe this anymore?" Taken by Mother Teresa's authentic way of living the faith, Claiborne and his friends decided to call to her mission in Calcutta to see if they could get an internship.

"I was expecting a polite, 'Missionaries of Charity, how can we help you?" Claiborne said. "And I heard this raspy, old voice go, 'Hello?" And I was thinking I have the wrong number and it's $4 a minute. So, I started talking really fast. I'm like, "We're trying to get hold of the Missionaries or Charity or Mother Teresa's order out there, the Sisters." And she said, "Well, this is the Missionaries of Charity, this is Mother Teresa." And she said, "Yeah, come on out."

Claiborne said that in the streets and slums of Calcutta, he learned what it meant to stop complaining about the church in order to start becoming the church. Now as great a story as that is, you and I both have learned together that being salt and light in the world does not mean you have to pack up your stuff and move to Calcutta. We are called to be salt and light here, in this place.

Reflections of God's light into the cold world bring warmth and promises of healing. We carry the light into the world, fulfilling the righteousness demanded of loving God and the neighbor.

Jesus' words about salt and light described the way the church — the way you and I — are to be in the world. I believe you and I have learned that together. But it is hard work. It is exhausting, and at times we may be tempted to give up. We have tasted the zesty flavor of Christian community by holding hands and praying in hospital rooms. At times, the salt of our own tears has reminded us of God's faithful presence. And at other times, we have shared that healing, glowing light of God's love.

Time and time again this has been home to me in a straight-forward way when I am called to go on your behalf to have serious, one-on-one conversations with folks who do not come to church, but who in some way see this as their spiritual home. I can't understand how that works. But I know this: we are salt, and we are light, and it is through us the presence of Christ is incarnate.

Amen.

Uh-Oh

*In these "hard sayings of Jesus" Christians are called to
live wholeheartedly, led by the higher righteousness given
to us in love.*

Sometimes, I wonder what might happen in worship if instead
of saying, "Thanks be to God" after the reading of scripture,
the congregation would stand up and respond in unison by
saying, "What?" or "Yikes!" or "Uh-oh."

Jesus said, "You have heard that it was said to those of ancient times, 'You shall not murder'; but I say to you, if you
are angry with a brother or sister, you will be liable to judgment; and if you insult a brother or sister, you will be liable to
the council; and if you say, 'You fool,' you will be liable to the
hell of fire."

And...somewhere a congregation begins to twitch
nervously.

Jesus said, "You have heard that it was said, 'You shall not
commit adultery.' But I say to you that everyone who looks at
a woman with lust has already committed adultery with her in
his heart... "

And...at this point, several eyes begin to twitch. Sweat
begins to form on the brows of several present until someone
says, "uh-oh."

Jesus said "If your right hand causes you to sin, cut if off
and throw it away."

And...no one dares to stand up and say, "Thanks be to God."

Yet Jesus was not content to stop at either retaliation, con-
demnation, or amputation. He pushed even further down the

road of disquieting sayings: *I say to you* that anyone who divorces his wife, except on the ground of unchastity, causes her to commit adultery; and whoever marries a divorced woman commits adultery.

The congregation looks down at their feet.

Worship comes to a screeching halt, for no matter how many times the congregation has sung, "They will know we are Christians by our love," these hard sayings of Jesus stop us in our tracks.

The pause is even longer than twelve verses of "Just As I Am, Without One Plea."

As they say in the south, Jesus had moved from preaching to meddlin' and that creates a problem for us. Up to this point in the sermon on the Mount, Jesus' words felt as if they were healing balm to open wounds. Jesus' words have blessed the community, filling them with hope and extra helpings of grace. Jesus' words have brought comfort and peace.

But now he had increased the incline. The going was harder. This was faith without the frills, a leaner, more demanding path. His words picked up resistance as he trudged over the bumpy, uphill of life in Christian community. It's not easy. Anyone who has ever tried to get three or four kids to church on time understands what it means to get angry. Anyone who has ever taken a breath knows what it means to lust. Anyone who has ever been married knows how difficult it can be. The statistics speak for themselves: fifty percent of American marriages end in divorce.

Jesus pushed hard against the tide of the culture. He pushed the disciples further up the uneven path of faithfulness. Suddenly, we're not even sure if we want to bother moving forward.

As one scholar said, "Adultery. Lust. Plucking out an eye to avoid boarding the express train to hell. Preachers, welcome to Matthew 5:27-32!"[40]

Truth be told, there have been times when I have looked at these passages and have wished I could take a week of vacation. And I know that I am not alone in that. Several of my friends looked at me with blank expressions when I asked them for their ideas on Matthew 5:21-32. One of them said, "Try the Psalms."

Uh-oh.

My prayer today is that we engage these difficult words of Jesus wholeheartedly, because I believe that it is to our hearts that Jesus is speaking. His words are a balm for hearts that are weary and exhausted from toiling in a world were shame is valued more than grace, rage more than peace, and brokenness more than repair.

Jesus' contemporaries would have understood the heart not to be the seat of emotion but to rather be the center of action and conduct. The heart was the place of decision making and choice taking. Israel was called to love God with all its soul, with all its heart, and with all its strength. Earlier, Jesus offered the crowd this blessing: "Blessed are the pure in heart, for they shall see God." Jesus criticized our quest for material wealth by saying, "Where our treasure is, there will our heart be also." Alyce McKenzie pointed out that Jesus demanded that our hearts be pure and unblemished, "for out of the abundance of the heart, the mouth speaks."[41]

It is within the imagination of human hearts where on the one hand evil is contemplated, and where faithfulness is created.

40 Gary W. Charles, "Homiletical Perspective on Matthew 5:27–32," in *Feasting on the Gospels: Matthew*, Chapters 1–28, ed. Cynthia A. Jarvis and E. Elizabeth Johnson, First Edition, vol. 1, *A Feasting on the Word Commentary* (Louisville, KY: Westminster John Knox Press, 2013), 99.

41 See Alyce McKenzie, "The Telltale Heart: Reflections on Matthew 5:21-37" www.patheos.com, February 7, 2011.

These difficult verses are called the "six antitheses." They pose paradoxes and set up demanding choices as ways of describing the ways disciples are to live. These hard sayings are filled with hyperbole and can be difficult to understand. They seem impossible. It's like the scene in the classic "Home Alone" movie where the bad guy is standing the basement about to be pummeled by a bag of concrete. He sees it flying toward him and can only mutter, "Uh-oh."

Sometimes the most demanding words of scripture require us to think differently. Carol Howard Merritt told a story of an experience she had in college. She said there was someone in her dorm who was prone to nabbing other people's food from the dorm refrigerator. Time and time again someone would go out and bring home a doggy bag of leftovers for those weekend days when dorm food was less than desirable. More times than not, said Rev. Howard Merritt, that when she would go and open the refrigerator door the next day, she'd discover that the leftovers had been stolen, along with any other interesting items. This went on for several weeks, until "one particular morning." She continued: "I woke up and went into the kitchen to fetch some milk for my coffee, and I gasped. Someone had taped a sign to the refrigerator. In bold red letters, it said, "If your hand causes you to sin, 'Cut it off.'" Then, carefully taped to the sign was a fierce serrated-edge knife.

Uh-oh.

All of this took place, of course, within the confines of a fundamentalist Bible college. But even this absurd reading Matthew 5 rubbed a bit too close to home.

For some of us, the issue may be anger. In 21 years of ministry at Woodlawn, I have yet to knowingly encounter a murderer. Your secret is safe with me. If I ever see a Dateline reporter in the narthex, I will know that's changed. But I have known moments when out of control anger from my own life has inflicted mortal wounds on one of my siblings in Christ. Yet at the same time, there are moments when scripture calls us to be angry. There are times when anger is a creative way of igniting change. How do we handle this?

Or how do we extend Christian welcome and grace to those who have tried and tried and tried to make their marriage work, but to no avail? How is it that we create places where wounds can be healed? Time and time again I have heard stories of those whose guilt over filing for divorce from an abusive spouse has caused spiritual death within them. Indeed, how many times have we encountered those who have been told they are excluded from the sacraments of Christ because they are divorced?

Tom Long, by the way, reminded us that Jesus' words here direct us to see marriage in the context of Jesus' world, where women were considered property and men could seek a divorce relatively easily, though women could not. God sees marriage, said Long as a communion between two people that expresses the faithfulness of God. He noted, "In Jesus' day, the customs and practices were a direct assault on those values."

Jesus said: "Pay attention to your heart."

He challenged every structure of shame and called us to place the law of God within our hearts. Choose this way, he told us. It is the way of life. It is the way of abundance. It is the way of joy: you shall love the Lord your God with all your heart, with all your soul, and with all your mind, and you shall love your neighbor as yourself."

Those may be easier words to say, but they certainly lead us to considerations that can be painful and difficult. Afterall, when the holy dances with the ordinary, sometimes our very ordinary toes will get stepped on.

Amen.

Transfiguration Sunday

Matthew 17:1-9

Surrounded By Glory

After six days Jesus took with him Peter, James and John the brother of James, and led them up a high mountain by themselves. There he was transfigured before them. His face shone like the sun, and his clothes became as white as the light. (vv. 1-2)

Transfiguration Sunday closes out Epiphany with one more display of dazzling light and revelation of God's glory. The story is shared in Matthew, Mark, and Luke's gospel, and while each writer adds a particular twist, the basic story remains the same.

The accounts of Jesus' transfiguration all rely heavily on Moses' encounter with God in Exodus 24. Both are stories of transformation wrapped in layers of mystery, surrounded by the smoky clouds of God's surprising presence. Separated by centuries, both the disciples and Moses encounter God's glory on the mountain in ways that are filled with more pyrotechnics than any Super Bowl halftime show.

When it comes to Jesus' Transfiguration, we have a slight advantage over the disciples. We know how the story ends, while Peter, James, and John were clueless as they hiked up the mountain. Up, and up, they went. Where they were going, no one knows.

Hint: it was going to be epic.

We hear this story every year right before the beginning of Lent. It sometimes feels like Jesus was throwing his own version of a Mardi Gras party, minus the food, drink, and beads. Peter, James, and John would probably have preferred the food and drink. I have probably preached this text at least thirty times. This week I came to the astonishing conclusion that after all these years I still do not completely understand it.

So, I looked at ways that other preachers have approached this over the years. I found one sermon written in the 1990s where the preacher tried to use Disney movies like *Cinderella* and *The Lion King*, which was cute, but somehow not completely satisfying as I tried to imagine Peter, James, and John turned back into mice at midnight.

Another preacher took a different approach. He described looking at a newsletter that offered a suggestion on how to make "Transfiguration Sunday really come alive." The preacher said the newsletter suggested renting a portable fog machine, filling it with dry ice and then projecting photos of Moses, Elijah, and Jesus on a large screen behind the communion table. Then, the newsletter said, recruit someone with a big, booming voice to read the scripture.

The preacher continued reading the instructions, "As the scripture is read, at the appropriate moments turn off the slides of Moses and Elijah so that Jesus is left alone. Turn on the fog machine in sufficient time that the fog thickens behind the communion table. Then, the voice of the lay reader booms out of the cloud saying, 'This is my Son, my chosen, listen to him!' Then, finally, turn off the fog machine."

The preacher then added, "Here the instructions say, 'This is very important!'"

The preacher said he finally discarded this as an opener to his sermon, wondering if the fog machine might set off the smoke alarms and bring in the fire department. He was also worried about what sort of theological crisis would be set off if he asked a woman to read the voice of God, "This is my Son!" In the end, he let the account speak for itself.

It's not a bad idea. Up on the mountains, Jesus was surrounded by his inner circle. They hadn't a clue why they were there, but that was fine since they wouldn't understand anyway. In fact, the entire event was shrouded with a mystery as deep and thick as the cloud that surrounded them.

Surrounded by glory, the disciples were nonetheless confronted by mystery.

Nothing about this encounter made sense: not the hike up the mountains, not Jesus' transfiguration, not his dazzling brilliance, not Moses and Elijah casually strolling over from the Old Testament to chat with Jesus, and certainly not the cloud that overshadowed them. It is all a mystery, capped by God's voice calling to them, "This is my Son, whom I dearly love. Listen to him!"

God's words mirror what was spoken at Jesus' baptism, but this time they are not offered to Jesus, but to us. Confronted by all these mysteries, the disciples shrink back in fear, unable to move. What else do you do when you are confronted by mystery?

We reduce the power of this story if we try to explain it away with special effects. I am not confident enough in my stage skills to expect that filling the sanctuary with smoke would go well at all. I am even less confident that trying to make the unreasonable seem reasonable with special effects would ever convince someone that the Lord was speaking to them.

A long time ago, friends of my parents were struggling with their aging mother. It had become apparent that it was no longer safe for her to live at home, but Emma was a stubborn Scot. She was not having it. She told her daughter and son-in-law, "I am not moving from this house until the Lord tells me." When these friends of my parents shared this with their group of friends, one of them piped up and said, "Well, there's your answer. Stand outside her bedroom window early in the morning with a megaphone and say, "Emma! It's the Lord! It's time to go!"

Moments of mystery catch us by surprise. They are confusing and bewildering. Seldom do we find the answers we need, at least not immediately. So it is that Peter, confused by all that he has seen, decides that the time is ripe to start a building campaign. "Let's build a new sanctuary," Peter told Jesus, foreshadowing words forever echoed by church leaders. Confronted by mystery, we rush around instead of remaining still. "Don't just stand there," we say, "do something."

Confronted by mystery, we become afraid. How will we make it through this time of life? Why is this happening? What did I do to deserve this?

When we are confronted with mystery, shame, and inadequacy flood our being. Paralyzed by fear, we do exactly what Peter did — rush around trying to make sense of this mystery. Sensing it is a problem, we begin to look for solutions, any solutions. "Let's build a new building!" someone will say. "Let's get a bigger youth group!" another will add. "Let's start a fundraising drive!"

Afraid, disappointed, ashamed, are all ways of coping with the mystery we cannot understand.

But follow the story. Notice that when the mystery of the transfiguration sweeps over them, the only thing God told the disciples was to be quiet. If God had a Bronx accent, then these words would be translated something like, "Wouldya shut up already?"

Don't just do something, Peter. Stand there. Stand there in the cloud of my presence and listen to what Jesus is saying. Stand in the cloud I have sent as a shade, so that your eyes might be able to fully take in Jesus' dazzling brilliance. Stand there, and do not be afraid.

When mystery sweeps over us, when glory surrounds us, we may be prompted to rely on anxiety-driven thinking. We may impetuously respond, "Oh, my Lord! This is incredible! Let's bottle up this event so that everyone can experience it!" We may even think that God wants us to rush around and do something spectacular.

But notice what Jesus did. Transfigured into glory, surrounded by mystery, he moved close to the disciples, and he touched them. He offered comfort. He brought hope. He acted like he had always acted, trying to help them make sense of what was incomprehensible.

That is our good news: in terrifying moments of change where everything we know has been thrown up into the air, God greets us by name. God says to us, "Do not be afraid."

So here we are: gathered on the mountain, surrounded by signs of glory, wondering what it all means. Confronted by mystery, we are faced with trying to make sense of all of this.

Jason Reynolds' young adult novel *Long Way Down* is a story of a Black teenager named Will who was trying to come to grips with the murder of his big brother. When his brother was killed, Will recalled that he was taught three rules: Don't cry. Don't snitch. Get even. Will, who was a star student, went over to his brother's dresser. Inside was a gun that he had never touched. Will then set out to avenge his brother's death.

What followed was a mysterious sixty-second elevator ride that spanned over a hundred pages of text. As he got on the elevator, Will was joined by a mysterious person who was smoking a cigarette. This happened at each level, with the smoke growing at every stop. Each one of the people was an important person from Will's past — yet they were all long dead. They challenged him to rethink the rules. He coughed on the smoke. It stung his eyes, filled his lungs. I won't ruin the story, but at the end Will was confronted with a choice: would the transforming moment inside that elevator change him, or would he remain the same?

Surrounded by glory, we are confronted by mystery. But out of that mystery comes the good news that sets aside our fears. "This is my Son," God says to us, "Listen to him!"

Amen.